AMAZED
by
GOD'S GRACE

Overcoming Racial Divides by
the Power of the Holy Spirit

LARRY ONEY

D1431467

AMAZED
by
GOD'S GRACE

Overcoming Racial Divides by
the Power of the Holy Spirit

— LARRY ONEY —

Published by The Word Among Us Press
7115 Guilford Drive, Suite 100
Frederick, Maryland 21704
wau.org

22 21 20 19 18   1 2 3 4 5

ISBN: 978-1-59325-335-6
eISBN: 978-1-59325-510-7

Cover design by Suzanne Earl
Cover photo courtesy of Hope and Purpose Ministries

Made and printed in the United States of America

Library of Congress Control Number: 2017960701

Lovingly dedicated to Andi,

my most cherished friend.

Contents

DEAR READER,

I set out to tell the story of the journey of my faith, hoping to lift up the name of the Lord and his amazing grace. I especially want to give my own perspective on the power of God's love to overcome adversity, no matter what circumstances we currently face or have faced in the past. God's amazing grace is so expansive that it is like a great tree with room under its branches for all of his children.

As a black man, I can speak from experience about the realities of injustice, poverty, and struggle, but I can also speak from experience about the power of God's triumphant love and the amazing grace that he gives us throughout our lives as we journey to the house of the Father. Sometimes this outpouring of God's grace is imperceptible, but nonetheless, the weight of his glory still presses in upon us.

Larry

CHAPTER ONE

LIFE ON THE PLANTATION

I was seven years old when my life changed forever. During the early 1960s, on a cool, bright morning, I stuffed my lanky frame onto the open windowsill of our tiny house and pulled one knee up to my chin. Holes in my pants exposed freshly scabbed knees, and one dirt-crusted bare foot dangled in the slight breeze. I perched quietly, studying my dad—Clifton Oney—and the white land-owner standing in our yard.

I was rigid with curiosity because the landowner had actually gotten out of his truck. No landowner in the Louisiana Delta would make the effort to get out of his truck just to speak to a black sharecropper unless something serious or important was happening. They stood near the electric water pump that had been put in only days earlier, a replacement for the old hand pump. The dirt that had collected around the new installation was still fresh on the ground.

I watched the white man rest his hands on his hips. He appeared to be frustrated or annoyed about something. I saw his head tilt. He pushed his grey banded hat to one side. His clean white shirt reflected against the bright sun, making me squint. He was not talking ugly to my dad, but he was clearly letting him know what he expected and what he wanted.

Towering over the white landowner, my dad seemed to stand as tall as the sky. His powerful hands were impressive. I knew if he wanted to, he could snap a man in half. He had plenty of chances, though he never dared. One false move in front of a white man would have meant his life. Dad was tall, at least 6'4", but there was no question as to who was in charge and who held the power during this exchange.

My dad, known as "Bubba," held a subservient, humble posture in front of the property owner. Despite the immense difference in their sizes, their mannerisms told the story without words. However, words were spoken. From my window seat, I heard them. Those words etched themselves into my brain and dramatically influenced the rest of my life.

The white man spoke sternly. "Bubba, don't you let Bea take these boys away from here. I've been good to y'all." (Bea was my mother.) The white man heartlessly reminded my dad about some basic repairs done to the house to keep the wind from shooting through the bottom of the floor in the wintertime—repairs, like the new pump, meant to entice us to stay. It was clear that he did not want us boys taken off the land, since the eight of us were a significant source of labor.

The landowner knew that my mom wanted to move away from the plantation, but the landowner held the power, and he dictated to my dad not to let us leave. My dad could only say, "Yes, sa." Dad didn't have the power to resist the demands of the landowner, though my mom had other ideas.

My father was a survivor, and he knew his place. He grew up on the dicey edge of brutality, when a white man could legally beat a black man down to the ground for little or no reason. I am sure my dad's size caused him to know this misery firsthand. Being a large man made him a target of sorts. Any slight movement, or the smallest sign of defiance, could bring him harm or even death.

Looking back, I realize that race, and the power it allowed one group of people over another, swept forcefully into my awareness during that encounter in the yard. The fear, anxiety, and hatred that I came to know would only be washed away many years later, when God's amazing grace would help me to overcome race. Not that any of us ever completely overcome the pain and the indignity of one race asserting itself over another race, but each of us can make a decision with God's grace to forgive those who have hurt us in matters of race.

Stop judging by appearances, but judge justly. (John 7:24)

One of the things that helped me begin to change my thinking was the love and kindness, over time, of some of the people around me. The Letter to the Galatians, chapter five, lists love and kindness as fruits of the Spirit. We, as the body of Christ, need to exhibit these fruits in unspoken testimony to people who won't necessarily listen to a word from us. Instead, they will see our actions. Our loving kindness, our gentleness, and our self-control will be a very loud testimony to unbelievers, just as it was for me.

✿ God's Grace

Sometimes when a painful or traumatic event happens, you can become guarded and wary of others. The enemy wants you to feel alone and as if you cannot escape whatever trauma you are enduring. God, on the other hand, wants you to know that you are *not* alone and that he provides armor to equip you to withstand the arrows of the enemy (see Ephesians 6:11, 13-17). The taunts that people hurl at you like arrows will no longer hurt, because you can now see that those people are in pain themselves and do not know the truth. You can begin to feel empathy for your enemies and pray for them and their healing. God's grace allows you to feel compassion for others—even those who would hurt you.

Have you experienced a painful event in your life? How did God help you through it?

Do you put on the armor of God every day for protection? Why or why not?

How can you allow God's grace to change the way that you view challenging situations?

Put on the armor of God so that you may be able to stand firm against the tactics of the devil. (Ephesians 6:11)

CHAPTER TWO

WHAT'S IN A NAME?

My mother's name was Beatrice Allen, and she had thirteen children with my father, although two children died at birth. My parents were never married. All of my brothers and sisters have the last name of Allen. I am the only child with my father's last name, even though we all have the same father and mother.

My mother was not well after having me, so my dad had to go and register me with the parish—in Louisiana, counties are called parishes—in order for her to get medical care. My father only had a third-grade education, so he could sign his name, but that was all. He didn't understand that a child born to an unwed mother got the last name of the mother.

Therefore, I got my father's last name—Oney—but I used my mother's last name, Allen, until I reached the eighth grade. At that point, I had my heart set on playing sports, especially basketball. The school demanded a copy of my birth certificate, and when the school officials saw the name listed on it, I had to use my real last name, Oney, from then on. I've had to explain this all my life, sometimes with embarrassment.

For through faith you are all children of God in Christ Jesus. (Galatians 3:26)

✿ God's Grace

Our name represents who we are and often gives us a sense of self. Children are taught to "live up to your name" or "be proud of your name." Names are important. God calls us by name (see, for example, Isaiah 43:1; John 10:3).

Cherish your name, but remember that to God, you are more than your name. You must begin to see yourself as God sees you, because this is who you truly are. You might see all of your flaws, yet when God looks at you, he sees your heart. Yes, God does see the physical parts of you, but he created you in his own image. To God, you are beautiful and unique.

God is not color-blind. God loves color! Whatever color you are, he chose to create you as a beautiful human being. To God, each human is a work of art, and he is the artist.

Do you see yourself as God's work of art, or do you focus on your flaws? Do you tend to be harshly self-critical, or are you perhaps too self-satisfied? How does your self-appraisal strengthen or undermine your ability to talk to people about God's love for them?

Take some time in prayer to think about these questions. Ask God to help you see yourself as the work of art that you are so that you can communicate his love to others.

CHAPTER THREE

FAMILY

The leader of the family, indisputably, was my oldest brother, A. C., and then my next brother, Cliff. After that it would be George. Both Cliff and George are ordained ministers today; Cliff is a Pentecostal minister, and George is a Baptist minister. Our family was a loving family, but my father was somewhat removed. I didn't understand why my dad was gone so much, and I was angry with him for not being present enough during my childhood.

My dad was a very hard worker and well known on the plantation. Even though he was a tractor driver (a coveted role on the plantation), he made my mom starch and iron his pants every day. She used the old type of starch that she had to mix before ironing. Dad always went to work looking crisp and always returned home dirty. He wore a cap on the top of his head. For some reason, he was very particular about how he looked when he started the workday.

I don't remember my parents having much fun. I remember the tension about the lack of money and not having enough to eat. I wish I could say that my parents were nurturing, but I never felt like I was nurtured—certainly not by my father and not very much by my mother. In fact, I don't remember my mother holding me very often. Our family was just too large, and there was little time for anything but work.

My mom was short in stature but tall in wisdom. She was a beautiful woman, one-quarter Cherokee Indian with a full head of coarse black hair. She was very gracious. I guess everybody thinks that their mom is beautiful, and I am no exception. Even though she only had a fifth-grade education, she was very smart.

I remember hearing my mom, when I was a young person, praying out loud and crying out loud to God. I had no real concept of God as a six- or seven-year-old, but I knew, when I heard my mom praying, that something very serious was going on. Whenever we heard Mom praying, no one would go into the room to interrupt her. Sometimes Mom would just take herself away and be in her room, and even if she wasn't praying out loud, we knew she was in prayer. Even when I was a teenager, I was impressed by her prayerfulness.

Toward the end of her life, my mom and I were very close. We spoke not so much as mother and son but as two people on a spiritual path. She was the matriarch and the strength of our family. I knew that she loved me. She was a prayerful woman, but I knew that there was a lot of pain in her life.

My brothers James and Bobby were the ones I looked up to when I was young. They were closest to me in age, and it seemed as if they could do almost anything. I often felt inconsequential as a young child because there were so many of us, and it seemed as if I was never able to do what the older kids were doing.

One time in particular, I remember standing on the porch watching my older brother climb into his old blue car. Several others stuffed themselves into the vehicle until the car was full. I wanted to go too, but they all laughed and said I was too young to go for a ride. I had to stay behind.

He found them in a wilderness,
a wasteland of howling desert.
He shielded them, cared for them,
guarded them as the apple of his eye. (Deuteronomy 32:10)

Whether you grew up in a loving home with both parents or were raised by only one parent or someone other than a parent, God wants you to come to him. As you grow in your faith, God becomes your true Father—a parent who loves you and will not abandon you. You are truly a child of God. (See Ephesians 1:3-8; 2 Corinthians 6:17-18; 1 John 3:1; and Romans 8:17.)

As a child of God, you are free to go to him at any time and speak with him about your life, your needs, and your desires, knowing that God wants to give you good things, as a loving Father would. God has a good future planned for you, and he is waiting for you to come to him and discuss it with him. As a child of God, you can find your hope and your freedom.

Do you view God as a loving father? Do you believe that as a mother cares for her baby, God will never be without tenderness for you (see Isaiah 49:15)? What experiences from your own childhood are holding you back from trusting in God? What experiences encourage you? Do you feel confident that God will not abandon you?

Earthly parents are not perfect, but God is. Bring your memories to him, and discuss them with him in prayer today.

See what love the Father has bestowed on us that we may be called the children of God. Yet so we are. The reason the world does not know us is that it did not know him. (1 John 3:1)

🌸

CHAPTER FOUR

LIVING IN EGYPT

Sharecroppers never owned any of the land or houses where they worked, and we were no different. Our house belonged to the plantation owner. The landowners dominated the sharecroppers, controlling the amount of food available, the hours we worked, and where we lived. Though we lived in rural northern Louisiana, it was as if we were living in Egypt.

The undeniable, unavoidable chains of bondage held me, my family, and all the black folk around us. It felt as though we were simply manacled puppets and the white landowners pulled the strings, *those invisible chains*, as they pleased. There was no regard for age or sex. Men and women, young and old, were manipulated within the carefully crafted structure of the sharecropper economy.

For black people, sharecropping was the way of life in the Deep South during the early 1960s. The physical shackles of subjugation had long since been removed from my ancestors; however, the emotional and psychological bondage of enslavement was still clearly present. My family lived on Hollybrook Plantation, which I now refer to as Egypt. All of us who worked the land at Hollybrook found ourselves swallowed up by racism, intimidation, and hopelessness.

We lived down a long road from the main highway. Way Way Lane was a very dusty, hard gravel road. You could see someone coming from a long way off. A cloud of grit flared with each approaching vehicle. Our house was nothing more than a shack with tar paper on the outside. The little structure held all of us— my parents, eight boys, and three girls.

When it was time to eat, everybody knew it, and my mother didn't need to call us twice. If a younger child didn't eat quickly enough, the older kids would eat whatever was on that person's plate. You came hungry, and you ate as fast as you could. There was no forcing anybody to eat leftovers. In our house, there was no such thing as leftovers. I was at least thirty years old before I learned to slow down and eat at a normal pace.

There was no indoor plumbing at all. Our house was the same as most, except that we had the small electric pump in the yard instead of the regular hand-crank pump the other families had to use. Our electric pump was an enticement, because we provided so many laborers for the field. Even though that pump was not anything fancy and was outside, it was considered a luxury and was a big help to us. But whenever I saw the pump, it was a sore reminder of the landowner's domination, of his attempt to keep my father and us boys on the land.

The younger children shared a room, and the older children shared a room. Our bedrooms were walled with thin partitions painted a loud blue. We slept crammed at both ends of the bed, some of us toward the head and some toward the foot. Sleeping in the oppressively hot summer weather was almost impossible, but in the winter, we were glad for the extra body heat.

Our beds consisted of the sack material that was used for hauling cotton. The sacks were sewn together, and cotton from the fields was stuffed inside, creating a mattress. Every morning we had to toss the cotton around inside the mattress to freshen it up. It was not a pretty sight. We always slept with some kind of bugs in the bed, flakes of dried earth from the fields, and God only knows what else. If there was any bed-wetting or anything like that, the sack-filled cotton bedding was fluffed up and turned over.

My mom was too busy—after working in the fields, feeding eleven kids, and taking care of a husband—to do any more than she did. Some evenings we had a bath, and others we went to bed dirty.

Life on the plantation was not all bad. Like other children, I was always looking for things to do when I wasn't working in the fields. I loved jumping off the porch. It was the closest thing to flying. When Momma made me sweep the porch, I usually found myself swept up with the idea of flying, not cleaning. I always tried to see if I could jump farther than the day before.

Once I climbed up on the tall shed where my dad kept his spotless black Chevy Impala. It seemed as if I was several stories up, and I was scared to death. When I jumped off, I felt like I was in the air forever. I landed shaken but with no broken bones.

I never went up on that shed again. That ended my obsession with flight.

Who are these that fly along like a cloud,
  like doves to their cotes? (Isaiah 60:8)

✿ God's Grace

Have you ever felt dominated or oppressed? Being controlled by someone else, even in a game, can be a frightening experience. As you begin to know Jesus, you will begin to realize that you are free.

Some people associate Jesus with more rules, yet the truth is that with Jesus, there is true freedom. You are free to be healed of your past, you are free to believe in a better future for yourself and your family, and you are free to become the person you were meant to be, as God created you to be before sin.

This may not be an overnight process, but Jesus will begin to heal you from your pain and disappointments the moment you come to him. Jesus is always gentle, and he heals you at your own pace. Some issues may take more time to heal because they're so traumatic or because they've been a part of your life for so long. Jesus won't rush you in the healing process. He understands that some things take time to truly heal, and he wants to make sure that you are fully healed and that you find true freedom in him.

Have you brought your pain and brokenness to the Lord? Have you given him full freedom to lead you to greater healing—or have you set restrictions on his work in your life?

Tell him that you surrender to him, moment by moment, trusting that he will lead you to full freedom, even as you continue to heal from whatever brokenness you have experienced in your life.

CHAPTER FIVE

THE GARDEN AND TREATS

Every house on the plantation had a garden. Sharecropper families would not have been able to make it through the winters without one. My mother canned everything she could from that garden so that we could have vegetables during the cold months. In our little garden, we grew corn, tomatoes, sweet potatoes, butter beans, snap beans, and all sorts of vegetables. *I have eaten my share of vegetables to last me a lifetime!*

My brothers and I supplemented the winter stockpile by seining small fish and freezing them. Cleaning, gutting, and freezing the fish was a messy job, but we couldn't rely on the garden alone, and it was nice to have something besides vegetables. We also got the supplemental "commodity food" that the government gave to poor families. We were very, very happy to get that food.

Everybody had chores, like feeding the occasional cow, pigs, and goats that we owned. In the wintertime, we collected wood and sticks, cut the wood, and hauled it inside for the stove. Everybody had something to do.

With so little variety in our food, I always knew what we were going to eat. A meal was usually a pan of flatbread and beans—white beans, butter beans, or some other kind of beans. During the summer—just as in the winter!—we ate more vegetables than I care to remember. The only time we got fruit was when my cousins came to visit us from the New Orleans area. They'd bring us oranges and apples, like manna from heaven.

Almost every Sunday, we would go visit "Ma," my dad's mother, who also lived on the plantation. Whenever we went to visit anyone, we were told that we should never ask for anything to eat. If we were offered food, we had to turn it down. But Ma never asked if we were hungry; she would just give us something to eat.

Ma was a great and gentle woman who sold little boxes of candy. People would walk a mile or two just to buy her five-cent candy, but she never allowed my family to buy any, knowing we didn't have money for luxuries. Before we left her house, however, Ma would always make sure that all of us got a three-colored piece of flat candy for free. I have fond memories of Ma and the nice smile on her face.

One time my mother allowed me to go with her and my dad to the grocery store. There was a lady working behind the counter, cutting sandwiches into nice perfect little squares. I didn't dare ask for anything, but I did make several passes in front of her, attempting to get her attention. I succeeded.

I got to try one of those delicious-looking sandwiches she had created, prepared with an incredible yellow creamy substance. For the first time in my life, I had a store-bought sandwich with mustard on it. I had never tasted mustard before, and it was the most amazing thing!

> *"Go, eat rich foods and drink sweet drinks, and allot portions to those who had nothing prepared; for today is holy to our LORD. Do not be saddened this day, for rejoicing in the LORD is your strength!"(Nehemiah 8:10)*

✹ *God's Grace*

When the devil tempted Jesus in the wilderness, the first temptation dealt with food. Jesus hadn't eaten for forty days, and he was hungry. Yet rather than fall for the devil's tactics, Jesus pointed out that man does not live by bread alone but by the Word of God. Just so, God wants to provide for all of your needs, spiritual as well as physical. He wants the best for you.

Turn to the Lord, and ask him not only to meet your needs but to use you today to meet the needs of someone else, perhaps someone you encounter as you go about your day's business. Pray for a specific opportunity—big or small, a physical need or a spiritual need—and ask the Holy Spirit to help you recognize it. Begin to make this type of prayer a daily habit so that you can bring God's love to others in concrete ways every day.

Filled with the holy Spirit, Jesus returned from the Jordan and was led by the Spirit into the desert for forty days, to be tempted by the devil. He ate nothing during those days, and when they were over he was hungry. The devil said to him, "If you are the Son of God, command this stone to become bread." Jesus answered him, "It is written, 'One does not live by bread alone.'" (Luke 4:1-4)

Chapter Six

School

Clothes were mostly hand-me-downs from child to child; we rarely had clothes that were new. I found it particularly humiliating when I had to wear shoes stuffed with paper because the shoes had holes in them. Even worse was the lack of a belt. When I went to school, I had to put a stick in my pants that twisted over loop to loop. If I didn't use a stick, my pants fell down.

There was a boy at school named Henry Lee who always liked to wrestle at recess, but I didn't like to because I thought somebody would see the stick in my pants. I got around it each time by finding the perfect little stick, one that wouldn't poke or hurt me but would still keep my pants up. Having paper in my shoes and a stick in my pants was not fun.

Nevertheless, I really liked going to school; I knew there was going to be food there. There was no such thing as "free lunch" when I was in school. Ms. Clay, a kind and wonderful woman, was one of my teachers and did so much for me during that time. If someone couldn't afford the ten-cent lunch, she would speak to the people in the cafeteria ahead of time, telling them to put some of her food on this person's or that person's plate. In this way, nobody would know when someone couldn't afford lunch. Ms. Clay did that for me every day of the year that I was in her class. She was a woman of mercy, sharing her food while guarding the dignity of young poor people.

I knew we were poor because we went to school with a friend named Kenneth who always had nice clothes, was very confident, and got a haircut every month. We only got haircuts every six months. Kenneth always looked fresh and wore good shoes. He could buy a soda anytime he wanted to. I thought Kenneth was rich!

All that black kids could look forward to after graduating high school was working the fields. That meant either chopping and picking cotton or climbing on a tractor to spread the poisonous chemical fertilizer and to turn over the dirt. Driving a tractor meant getting away from the sharp spikes on the cotton plants and not hunching and stooping all day. It was all we could hope for, although there was also the possibility, for a very few, of becoming the paymaster. Instead of chopping and picking cotton or handling poison and turning dirt, those who reached the paymaster position would pay out the nickels and dimes, or the two cents a pound, the cotton pickers earned during the summer months.

When you call me, and come and pray to me, I will listen to you. When you look for me, you will find me. Yes, when you seek me with all your heart, I will let you find me . . . and I will change your lot. (Jeremiah 29:12-14a)

✿ *God's Grace*

Every person is priceless to God, no matter how much money he has or what kind of clothes she wears. It can be hard to see that—we often judge others based on appearances and reject them if they don't meet our standard.

Have you ever done that? Did you feel an inner pricking of your conscience when you did? Did you take that judgment and rejection to God in the sacrament of confession? Ask the Holy Spirit to help you do a spiritual review of times when you might have judged harshly, and then resolve to avoid this sin in the future.

We are all precious to God. When God looks at us, he doesn't see our clothes or the size of our wallet or whether we are socially "acceptable." He sees a prince or princess of the kingdom of God. There is no higher rank that we could achieve. We who know Christ are heirs in the kingdom, and we are called to help others discover their true worth in him. You have been clothed by God; you are ready to go forth in his name (see Isaiah 61:10-11).

For through faith you are all children of God in Christ Jesus. For all of you who were baptized into Christ have clothed yourselves with Christ. (Galatians 3:26-27)

CHAPTER SEVEN

WORK AND PLAY

My life as a youngster seemed primarily centered on struggling to have enough to eat and on long hours of hard work. It didn't matter whether you were a boy or a girl, when you reached age seven, you went to the fields. When my turn came, I was anxious because, being so young, I didn't know what was expected of me. I had never picked or chopped cotton before. Chopping cotton involved removing the weeds from around the plants with a hoe, often in rock-hard dirt.

Every morning during the chopping season, the driver would pick us up on the truck while it was still dark so that we could be at the field at the break of day. We couldn't start chopping the cotton before daylight—we needed to be able to distinguish the weeds from the plants. In the dark, the men and older boys would sharpen the hoes; the grating sound of steel on steel made me tense and anxious. They tossed the hoes upside down into a box situated at the back of the truck, where the hoes rattled around in the blackness.

The driver would already have the ice for the community water bucket. In the pitch dark, I could hear the sound of the block of ice hitting the bucket. Grasshoppers, crickets, and frogs echoed against the noise. The darkness held millions of insects that sounded like an orchestra of clicking, chirping, and whistling.

Everybody was quiet in the morning. It was eerie as a child to be on the back of the truck going to the field. I didn't know where I was going. I didn't know how far it would be. I was just plain scared! The first couple of days that I went out were the scariest. I had no idea where I was; everything seemed huge. I was with adults that I hadn't been around before. Nobody was paying attention to me; I was on my own and learned how to chop cotton by doing it. I learned to pick cotton the same way. I would put it in the sack and drag it to the paymaster staging area that was stationed somewhere at the end of one of the rows.

Everybody was in the field. The women would have rags around their heads, and the men mostly wore hats. Even in the summer, we all wore long sleeves to keep the sharp cotton boughs from slicing our skin and the chemicals from getting on our arms. Many of us had rashes and medical problems from our constant exposure to the chemicals.

The rows of soybeans and cotton appeared to go on forever. To my young eyes, those rows looked as if they were miles and miles long. I remember thinking that there was no way I would ever finish one row. I still don't know how I did.

I can certainly understand how the Israelites felt down in Egypt. Their work seemed to have no end, and our work seemed to have no end. I had to pick a lot of cotton. Looking at the big trailer filled with the white fluffy bounty was intimidating. At age seven, I was too small to empty my own sack and had to get somebody to empty it for me.

If I picked fifty pounds, I'd get one dollar. The problem with getting one dollar at the end of the day was that I actually ended up with only around sixty cents for all of my work. I had no food to bring to the field, so I bought lunch from people who sold food in the fields. I could buy a soft drink and a sandwich, which was a piece of meat and some bread, for forty cents.

I didn't like chopping cotton. I didn't like having constant painful cuts and scabs. I didn't like being poor.

While working, I sometimes dreamed of playing. We played with the old tires from tractors that were in the fields. Our swimming pool was the irrigation runoff ditch at the end of the fields, where the poisonous chemicals gathered in odd-looking colors. It was a dangerous pastime, but it was our only escape from the heat and the bitterness we felt toward the white landowners.

But as it is written:
"What eye has not seen, and ear has not heard,
*   and what has not entered the human heart,*
*   what God has prepared for those who love him."*
(1 Corinthians 2:9)

❦ *God's Grace*

When you're in a difficult situation, it's easy to become bitter about it or about the people responsible for your suffering. It's important to deal with your bitterness right away through prayer. Bitterness can cut off your view of God or make you feel alienated from him if you let the bitterness grow. Questions like "Where is God when I need him?" can invade your thinking.

Bitterness can also cause a person to feel cut off from friends, family, or the Church. This is what the enemy wants: Satan wants you to feel cut off and alone, full of bitterness and anger.

Learning to forgive those involved in your difficult circumstances can be very healing. We have all lived through situations that have stirred up bitterness within us. Whatever your circumstances, have you brought them to the Lord in prayer? If possible and appropriate, have you talked with those who caused your suffering? Or have you just buried your pain and moved on?

Let the Lord shine his healing light on you. With Jesus' help, the bitterness and disappointment you have suffered don't have to have a stranglehold on you for the rest of your life. You can be set free!

CHAPTER EIGHT

HELP AND ENCOURAGEMENT

In the morning when we hit the fields, the women would be singing. I didn't get it at all. Yet before I had any spiritual basis for understanding, I knew in my being that this singing was something special— something deep and triumphant—even if I didn't understand why.

The one song that I remember is "I'll Fly Away." The women sang soulfully, sounding more like "I Fly Away." But I was confused. To my mind, the cotton balls were like tiny clouds in a briar patch. Flying away was supposed to bring freedom, but among those endless rows, freedom was a far-reaching dream.

While the women sang, everybody else who was working would be quiet. It was as if the others were respectful of the singing or maybe pondering the words and the idea of flying away from bondage.

The women would sing in the morning, but during the sweat of the day, during the break, there would be no singing; everybody was very businesslike. When their voices switched off in the hot air, the loud noise of hidden insects rang free. As dusk crept in and the work was almost over, the singers would start in again.

In the beginning, I felt a hardness toward some of the singing. What is there to sing about? This was a bad deal. I didn't understand the complexity of flying away at such a young age. I now understand that they believed that the Lord was literally going to come and snatch them up and away from their work, from the sweat, and from the heat. They believed they were going to be caught up in the air, in the beautiful blue sky.

If you were a child working in a long row chopping cotton, the women would come and help, singing. It was a beautiful thing when I think of it today. The singers held their heads high because they were singing a song of victory. It was a song of death and yet of God's love overcoming death and overcoming everything that they were going through. Still, I wasn't even sure who or what God was.

Later on, when the old people who went through the Jim Crow era and segregation sang that song, you knew it came from a deep place. They were testifying to God's delivering them out of evil, torturous situations. I didn't know until much later all that they had been through. They held on to their secret dignity, which nobody could take away.

After I became a Christian, I understood. It was then that I wanted to hear Mom sing "I'll Fly Away." She could sing! Once, over a period of three or four hours, I kept saying, "Mom, would you sing it again? Would you sing it again?" I seemed to enter into that song, into the spirit of those words.

Whenever I hear that song today, it is a source of encouragement. I didn't understand for a long time, but in a way, I was kind of like John Newton, the author of "Amazing Grace." I was blind, but now I could see.

Sing out, heavens, and rejoice, earth,
 break forth into song, you mountains,
For the LORD comforts his people
 and shows mercy to his afflicted. (Isaiah 49:13)

❀ God's Grace

Sometimes the work and toil that you do on this earth can seem neverending, especially when it involves hard labor with little choice or reward. As a Christian, you know that you are called to work hard while on this earth, but you also know that ultimately, God will reward you. Remember: your reward is from God, not man. So if you must deal with no thanks, little pay, or discouraging circumstances, you can be assured that this life is temporary and that God, your Father, will give you your true reward. Songs like "I'll Fly Away" help to remind us of this truth during the darkest of times.

Still, God does not call us to be passive. And especially when we can help relieve the sufferings of others, we must not be passive. If you are an employer, are you paying a just wage and caring for your employees? If you are a worker, are you diligent about your work? Whatever your role, you have a responsibility to live according to the demands of the gospel.

Pause now to read about the separation of the sheep and the goats when God comes to judge us at the end of time (see Matthew 25:31-46). Ask yourself if you are passively drifting through this life or if you are actively meeting the demands of the gospel.

If you are actively serving the gospel, then whatever you must survive on this earth, your eternal reward is waiting. There will be a time of rest and refreshment, a time to sit at your Father's table and feast, and an eternity to live with God, singing of his unfailing grace and mercy!

"Come to me, all you who labor and are burdened, and I will give you rest." (Matthew 11:28)

CHAPTER NINE

MOURNING ON THE "MORNING" BENCH

I went to church only a few times as a youngster. The little Baptist church near us had something called the "morning" bench inside the church, or so I thought. It was, in fact, the *mourning* bench. This was the bench where you could go and seek God.

Even young kids were expected to sit on this bench and seek God. One evening I went to the mourning bench service and found everybody crying with heavy emotion. The adults were all saying, "Look for a sign!" I thought it was all strange. Frankly, I thought the whole thing about God was just hocus-pocus.

People reported seeing signs in the sky, like six stars aligned in layers, or they saw the moon dance or something. I didn't see anything. I wasn't buying it; I wasn't getting it. Nonetheless, I sat on the mourning bench. I tried to seek God the best I knew, but I felt nothing. I put some spit on my eyes to make it appear that I had been crying so that people would see that I had indeed sought God.

> The LORD is near to all who call upon him,
>   to all who call upon him in truth. (Psalm 145:18)

❀ God's Grace

Jesus invited children to come to him and even got mad at those who tried to stop the children from coming. While children may not be able to sit still for hours listening to a teaching, they can and will sit for a reasonable time to learn about Jesus and God's love. And not only do they learn from us, but we can learn from them. Having a childlike faith is important for a Christian.

Having childlike faith means that you listen with eagerness, that you ask questions and wonder about things, and that you go to Jesus about everything. It can also mean that when you hear God's truth, you recognize it, believe it, and live by it.

How is your childlike faith? Are you as eager as you once were for the things of God? Are you curious? Do you ask questions, or does your fear hold you back? Once you know one of God's truths, do you live by that truth?

Pray for childlike faith today.

Jesus said, "Let the children come to me, and do not prevent them; for the kingdom of heaven belongs to such as these." (Matthew 19:14)

CHAPTER TEN

DETERMINATION

My parents didn't rant about being poor. It was just kind of, this was life, and you did what you could. My mom, however, had apparently gotten a taste of a different life, maybe when she went to visit her sister in the New Orleans area. At any rate, she saw another way of living, and one day, something was stirring. Momma was talking about moving. She had set her mind on delivering her children from life on the plantation.

Moving brought up fears and a sense of instability in me because all I had ever known was living in our little house. It was a nervous time when she talked about bringing us out of Hollybrook.

I remember my mother saying, "I'm gonna getch y' all outta here. I don't want y'all to grow up like this." The boldness in her voice sent a clear signal that life was about to change. She was a very frank and direct person, not at all fearful. She wasn't afraid of white people, of men, or of anything. Momma had been through a lot and had seen a lot and was stronger and more confident for all of it.

Determined to make a better life for us, my mom decided we were moving to Kenner, Louisiana, a suburb of New Orleans. She started moving us out in groups, taking the oldest boys first. Clifton, A. C., and George had to find work because they needed to secure housing for all of us. I had to stay back in the country with my older sister, who was put in charge, and my younger brothers and sisters. Mom didn't come to get us for almost a year, and my dad was rarely home. That was a horrible time. I continued to work in the field while my sister cooked all the meals and tended to us all by herself.

It was a troubling experience for me, especially not knowing what was going to happen next. I was filled with fear and anger, and I cried a lot, but I didn't let anybody see me crying. I know my sister was afraid too, but she did the best she could—she was now the "momma." She tried to make sure we had something to bring to the field to eat. And sometimes, when we were able to save a little extra money, she would bake a caramel cake. My sister was a good cook!

The LORD said to Abram: Go forth from your land, your relatives, and from your father's house to a land that I will show you. (Genesis 12:1)

Finally, the day came when it was my turn to leave the country. I was about ten years old. I left with my mom, Uncle James, my sisters—Dora, Helen, and Alice—and my two younger brothers, Jimmy and Paris. Sadly, James and Bobby, two of my older brothers, did not join the family in Kenner for another two years because there was no work for them yet.

At the time, there was tension in the air at the edge of the Civil Rights Movement. I was aware that something was going on with Dr. Martin Luther King, Jr., and his marching. Dr. King had gone beyond what most black people in the Deep South could ever hope to escape—constant fear that whites were going to do them some harm. Dr. King's words "I am not afraid" rang in my mind.

Uncle James was very kind to come and bring us to the New Orleans area. He had a truck, packed the whole bunch of us in, and ordered us to stay low: "You have to keep yo' heads down goin' through Mississippi, cuz white folk will drag you out of the truck, and it's gonna be trouble. We can't have a bunch of nappy-headed children sticking their heads up when we go through Mississippi."

I wondered why we had to keep our heads down. I tried to imagine what would happen if we did get stopped. Is somebody going to be killed? Am *I* going to be killed? Are they going to kill my uncle? Are they going to kill my mom? I was scared to death on that trip, even though we were not stopped even once on the long ride.

During that era, there were a lot of unspoken rules that applied to black people. For example, it was understood that no more than one or two black males could be in a truck at one time. And blacks understood that we were not to look white people in the eye. It would be perceived as a threat that would bring immediate physical violence or, at the very least, a stiff reprimand. Many whites would have considered this as defiance—as if we were staring them down.

My mom brought us out of the bondage of plantation life. She was like our Moses. She was our deliverer. The long trip from Hollybrook to Kenner was hectic, but we made it safely. After the agonizing excursion, I thought that I had escaped the oppressiveness of race and prejudice. Instead, I came to learn of a new, more sophisticated apartheid system.

God is our refuge and our strength,
  an ever-present help in distress. (Psalm 46:2)

❀ God's Grace

When life seems hopeless, God is there to give us hope. God is present to be our strength and to help us hold on and have the courage to stretch ourselves for the good of others. When we are weak, Jesus is our strength. He will carry us when we think that we cannot go any farther.

"Do not be afraid," Jesus said many times in the Gospels. Fear can be paralyzing; it can keep us from even trying. We are human, and there are things in this world that are terrifying and can cause us to doubt and lose faith if we are not careful. Prayer can help.

A habit of *daily* prayer is even better because it keeps us in communication with God. It helps us to remain firm in our faith and to grow in our understanding that we can trust God. Sometimes we just have to continue to repeat the truths that we have learned from God in order to have the courage and strength to see something through to the end.

There are many passages in Scripture that will encourage you to "fear not." You can do a search in the Bible, either online or with a concordance, to find these; but here are a few passages to get you started: Luke 5:10; 12:32; Matthew 10:26-31; 14:26-27; 17:6-7; 28:10; Romans 8:15. When you come across Scripture passages that encourage you, make them part of your daily Bible reading until they are embedded in your mind, and you can turn to them when you are afraid.

> *The LORD is my light and my salvation;*
> *whom should I fear?*
> *The LORD is my life's refuge;*
> *of whom should I be afraid? (Psalm 27:1)*

CHAPTER ELEVEN

NEW PLACES

I had the idea that in Kenner, everybody lived in mansions, like glass houses stacked on top of one another. I thought it would be just like *The Jetsons* cartoon. I imagined people floating around in cars in the air—that everything was just beautiful and perfect.

What I found instead was a new kind of separation and discrimination, with all the black people living in segregated neighborhoods apart from whites. It was just like on the plantation, except that the housing was much more expensive and a good deal smaller, and we had to pay rent.

Our large family all jammed into a three-and-a-half-room house on Milan Street that has since been torn down. All we had was a kitchen, a bathroom, and one bedroom. But I was not complaining. I could not believe there was a toilet that actually flushed—inside the house! This was a big deal. There were no more midnight races to the outhouse in total darkness. There was no more running as fast as you could through rain or cold. Now we just had to wait for the person in line ahead of us or endure the pounding on the door when someone demanded that we "hurry up!"

There was a sink in the kitchen, not a washtub, for washing the dishes. A bus took us to school, and not only did they give us something to eat for lunch, but we actually had a snack in the morning. There was food like I had never seen before—still very little at home but more food than we were used to. Even though things had not really changed for blacks, we had taken a tremendous leap from where we had been. I had never been in a house with a toilet inside of it. There was indoor plumbing. *Praise God!*

Despite the tension and anxiety, my mom wanted us to get a good education and have access to decent work. I called Kenner the Promised Land. Hollybrook, like Egypt, was a place where black people didn't have the right to express themselves at all. In the Promised Land of Kenner, black folk spoke up and moved about in cars. In Egypt, there was only enough money for basic survival. In the Promised Land, even though the housing was not much better, there were possibilities and hope. Even though this Promised Land was not flowing with milk and honey, it was a world away from the Egypt of the plantation.

Although Kenner offered better opportunities for me than Hollybrook Plantation, it was still scary. There was no one to nurture me or show me the ropes. There were swarms of people everywhere, and I no longer had the security of being around people I had known since birth. The city was a new experience with its many cars and houses, but there were also new threats, like drugs and guns. The general fear was in the unknown of this new place. However, I preferred this Promised Land that was not so perfect to Egypt.

My mom worked long hours, so again, she had no time to look after us children. The streets could very easily swallow you up. Mom was doing the best she could, but she had to make a living for us.

The LORD is good to those who wait for him,
*   a refuge on the day of distress,*
Taking care of those who look to him for protection.
(Nahum 1:7)

I was learning, in the Promised Land, that if people were willing to work hard, they would be paid decently for the work that they did. To go from making three dollars a day working sunup to sundown in the cotton fields to making five dollars before noon was a drastic change.

My job cutting grass with my cousin Nate went well for a while. I did most of the work. He told me what to do, since I was just the country boy. We got cash on the barrelhead. I made five dollars in just three or four hours. I was rich for the first time in my life!

The first time I was paid, I went right out to the K & B drugstore and bought myself a milk shake and a hamburger, fully dressed with pickles and mustard. I purchased them with my own money. It was wonderful. It was beautiful.

But it didn't last. After two years in Kenner, when I was about twelve years old, my job cutting grass slowed to nonexistent, and I had to go back to the plantation during the summer to work. Back at Hollybrook, I worked the fields, which allowed me to make a little money. I stayed with my Aunt Rosie B or, as we called her, "Roa-B." It was good to be with relatives, but I wanted to be with my own family in Kenner. I didn't see James and Bobby because they were at our old house, where my dad also lived.

I never dreamed I would end up back in the cotton fields, reenslaved in the bondage of Hollybrook Plantation. But there I was, back in Egypt. After a taste of life in the Promised Land, I hated the plantation more than ever. That first sight of those long rows made me homesick for the life I had left in Kenner. I missed my family and I missed my freedom, and I was really sad.

The worst job was chopping the weeds around the plants, because there were always little brown snakes between the rows. My cousins Freddie and Eddie would simply chop the snakes in two and keep working the rows.

Mom visited me on one occasion and rescued me from the fields after a day filled with dodging the countless brown snakes. (I am not a friend of snakes to this day.) She saw the misery I was going through and sent my brother A. C. the following week to bring me back to Kenner. He had no reverse on his car. I remained glued to my seat during the entire five-hour ride. Anything was better than dodging those snakes.

My dad came to stay with us, and it was one of the happiest months of my life. Life seemed to have some kind of order again. But Dad didn't stay long. One day he was just gone. We theorized among ourselves as to why he left so quickly and came up with all sorts of ideas. The glass plant where Dad worked was too hot. He longed for the open spaces in the country. He couldn't read. The traffic made him nervous. We thought up any reason why he would leave us.

🌸 God's Grace

As you try to help others, you begin to be part of the solution that raises people up from poverty or loneliness or depression or whatever ails them. Help can take many forms: some have a financial need, others may have a spiritual need. Children especially need attention; I certainly did as my family went through so many rapid and disorienting changes.

But young or old, we all need support and encouragement. As a child of God, you can look for opportunities to support and encourage others. Ask the Holy Spirit to give you a sensitivity to others—an inner quietness of spirit—so that you can tune in to their needs. Who may need a few minutes of your time? How can you encourage someone?

He will shelter you with his pinions,
and under his wings you may take refuge;
his faithfulness is a protecting shield.

*You shall not fear the terror of the night
nor the arrow that flies by day. (Psalm 91:4-5)*

CHAPTER TWELVE

WHO WILL YOU BE?

We all wonder what we'll be when we grow up, and I was no different in this regard, especially during my teenage years. The people who commanded the greatest respect in my neighborhood were teachers. And so as a young teenager, I thought I'd be a teacher, like Ms. Clay or Mr. Nero, whom everyone held in high regard. For a long time, I didn't have the confidence to share that dream with anyone or even let it come forth in my consciousness for too long.

I had other things on my mind in those years, including the racial prejudice I experienced on many occasions. The discussions in my neighborhood were primarily about racial prejudice—the unfairness and lack of respect of whites for blacks. There were marches and speeches on television, and for the first time, I understood what some of these messages were about. I was developing a consciousness about race and about racial structures, with their inequalities, indignities, and limitations.

The indignities took many forms. My mother, for example, cleaned and cooked for a white family who dropped her off far from her neighborhood to walk half a mile home after a full day's work because her neighborhood was deemed unsafe. Racial structural prejudice was everywhere. There was a store in Kenner, for example, that required black customers to purchase their items at a window around the back rather than allowing them to come into the store.

I began noticing things I hadn't noticed before. Our neighbors often teased us. It didn't matter that we were the same color as them.

They picked out our differences and made fun of us. We knew we sounded like a bunch of country bumpkins. They often said, "Y'all sound country" and "Y'all talk funny"—and I thought to myself, *Well, you guys sound funny too!*

On the plantation, everyone at least tried to get along and look out for one another. In Kenner it was a different story. I determined that I would learn to speak more clearly, but when I eventually learned to speak decent English, a peculiar thing happened. Some of the people in my neighborhood were negative about it. They said, "Well, you talk proper like white folks."

I wasn't sure if I should be glad or angry. Whatever I did, it seemed I wasn't good enough, that I didn't measure up to someone else's standards. Little by little, things began boiling inside me. A subtle rage was stewing in my gut. I had no idea how hot the flame would get or how much longer it would be before the pot boiled over.

When I was a freshman in high school, I finally resolved that I really didn't care what the black folk—and definitely not what the white folk—thought. I had no tolerance for any of it, especially for any real or perceived prejudice from whites. I was fertile ground for the anger growing inside of me.

For those who are led by the Spirit of God are children of God. For you did not receive a spirit of slavery to fall back into fear, but you received a spirit of adoption, through which we cry, "Abba, Father!" The Spirit itself bears witness with our spirit that we are children of God, and if children, then heirs, heirs of God and joint heirs with Christ, if only we suffer with him so that we may also be glorified with him. (Romans 8:14-17)

Unfortunately, there are people in this world who belittle others because they look different or sound different. But God is a God of beauty and variety, and he challenges you to embrace all of the shades of color that make up his creation.

> *I praise you, because I am wonderfully made;*
> *wonderful are your works!*
> *My very self you know. (Psalm 139:14)*

Whether or not you talk differently than someone else or look different, God says in his Word that you were created for a purpose: "For we are his handiwork, created in Christ Jesus for the good works that God has prepared in advance, that we should live in them" (Ephesians 2:10). Here's an excerpt from a prayer written by Cardinal John Henry Newman that makes the same point. I hope you will believe it and take it to heart.

> *God has created me to do him some definite service. He has committed some work to me which he has not committed to another. I have my mission—I never may know it in this life, but I shall be told it in the next. Somehow I am necessary for his purposes, as necessary in my place as an archangel in his.... I am a link in a chain, a bond of connection between persons. He has not created me for naught. I shall do good; I shall do his work. (Meditations and Devotions)*

🌸

CHAPTER THIRTEEN

HIGH SCHOOL AND STANDING UP

My brother James finally came to live with us in Kenner when I was in the ninth grade. He and I were close, and I was relieved and glad to have him back with us and away from the plantation. We were all together now, except for my dad.

As I grew, I began to get a feel for my neighborhood. This Promised Land was still hard. Widespread unemployment made life rough, not only for our family, but for most black families. The relentless undercurrent of crime forced us to be on guard in our surroundings. I felt the same insecurity and instability that I had felt on the plantation.

During this time, there was a lot of talk about Black Power. James Brown, a black musician, had a popular record that included the lyrics "Say it loud, I'm black and I'm proud." It was a time of black consciousness and pride, and many black people found his song uplifting. Change was coming. The black people in the neighborhood were developing a new sense of identity. A new identity started forming in me as well, along with a stronger sense of rebelliousness and a boiling defiance.

I decided that I wasn't going to be afraid of the police, who stopped people for no reason except that they were black in a white neighborhood—even if they were only there to cut the grass. As crazy as it sounds now, I was ready to die to fight these indignities. I was not only starting to talk about killing "blue-eyed devils" (white people); I also wanted to recruit others who shared my increasingly radical ideology.

In our poor neighborhood, there was a lot of strong talk on the street corners about white people. It was mostly "*The white man did this*" or "*The white man did that.*" It became an ever-present idea that the blacks should take up arms, fight for justice, and fight for rights. I was listening to a lot of that talk. It was everywhere, and I couldn't get away from it. And at the time, I didn't want to get away from it. It was shaping me into a militant young man.

I understand now the dynamics of what was happening, but at the time, lacking any real guidance, I found myself shifting dangerously fast toward the radical side. I listened to as much of the talk as I could and developed a deep animosity toward whites and the dominance they held over blacks. It was as if the Hollybrook landowner had followed us to Kenner and somehow multiplied himself. Now we were dominated by many instead of one.

The LORD is my light and my salvation;
    whom should I fear?
The LORD is my life's refuge;
    of whom should I be afraid? (Psalm 27:1)

I started high school just as the public schools in Louisiana were beginning to be integrated. John Martin High School, the black high school in Jefferson Parish, was closed down, and black kids were suddenly forced to go to East Jefferson High School in Metairie, the wealthiest parish in the state at the time. Needless to say, we were not welcomed at the new school. It was like a war zone, with blacks the enemy of whites and whites the enemy of blacks.

East Jefferson had over 3,000 students, but fewer than 250 were black. That was my first major encounter with a large number of white people. The blatant discrimination that I experienced and witnessed seemed endless, like the long, never-ending rows of cotton back on the plantation. Our principal seemed like a racist, as did some of the teachers I encountered. There was definitely no Ms. Clay at East Jefferson.

I was a good student, did my homework, and was a fast reader. High school wasn't a major challenge for me as far as learning went. I guess I did have some gift for retaining information because I didn't have great study habits. There was no desk or quiet place in our house where I could sit down and study.

As one of the few blacks in the ninth-grade class, I endured a particularly humiliating experience with one of my teachers. He demanded that I explain to the whole class why black people did certain things, including why more black people didn't work. I felt embarrassed and degraded by this teacher as he asked me questions in front of my entire class that I couldn't even begin to answer. I was very angry with him; I hated that man for what he put me through. He helped fan the flames of rage and black militancy in me, and for a very long time, I couldn't forgive him. It wasn't until I came to Christ years later that I was finally able to let go and forgive him.

I had a jacket with a Black Power fist on it, and I wore that jacket with pride and confidence. I was ready for any white person or authority figure to challenge me. I was growing strong in my convictions. I don't recall any of my siblings sharing my attitude about Black Power to the same extreme, certainly not my younger brothers. My older brothers were mostly caught up in their work.

The local sheriff said more than once that he would stop any and all blacks walking through white neighborhoods who had no business being there. There was national outrage, but nothing really happened to change things.

My brother James was a senior when I was a freshman. He had a job on Metairie Road, and though he was paid very little, he would always come and find me and give me a portion of whatever he had earned so that I could buy something to eat. If James hadn't helped me out, on many days I would've gone to basketball practice on an empty stomach. I was a starter on the team, loved the game, and played hard. Basketball was a good outlet for me, allowing me to let out some of my frustration.

James encouraged me in sports. I don't know how I would have made it without his devotion to my well-being. My dad was not in my life; in a way, James took his place. At least that was how I felt at the time.

Do not fear: I am with you;
 do not be anxious: I am your God.
I will strengthen you, I will help you,
 I will uphold you with my victorious right hand.
(Isaiah 41:10)

In my freshman and sophomore years of high school, I became the leader of a protest group of about fifty students, all black. I wasn't exactly clear on what we were protesting, but my attitude certainly grew out of the prevailing atmosphere of racial injustice and racial prejudice. For a while, I even boycotted the basketball team that I played on. I wasn't going to stand by and let whites or the white establishment (the principal, the coaches, and the teachers) dictate my life any longer.

The school principal believed that the majority rules on all counts. He respected only whites; he had no respect for the welfare or dignity of any other race. Even though the principal and I discussed things sometimes, nothing changed. During the school day, I wasn't allowed to wear my Black Power jacket with its clenched fist and torn-out sleeves. But whenever there was a home football game, I wore that jacket to let the principal know that I saw him as the enemy and that he and I were at war.

I led various marches and protests of unfair treatment toward black students. No one stepped up to help us. Once, when I called for a protest march over the racism at East Jefferson, I announced my plans to the television stations. They showed up to film us with our posters and banners. I told the principal that there was going to be an armed conflict, and he threatened to have me arrested, but he didn't.

I wasn't afraid of going to jail because I knew deep within that I had to stand up against the injustice we were enduring. I picked my words just as I had picked cotton. No one led me by the hand, and no one showed me what to do.

The principal and I understood one another. It was a power struggle, and he held all the power. But I had no fear of him. He was very cautious of me and made sure the assistant principals kept an eye on me.

For you were called for freedom, brothers. But do not use this freedom as an opportunity for the flesh; rather, serve one another through love. (Galatians 5:13)

I don't know how my mom felt about my militancy. She didn't go marching around the house saying, "Say it loud, I'm black and I'm proud" or anything like that, but she clearly understood indignity and unfairness because she had experienced it many times herself.

Mom had to meet with the principal on one occasion, when he threatened to suspend me for protesting and exhorting the other students to protest instead of going to class. Coming to the school cut into Mom's workday and was a hardship for her. My older brother Cliff took off work and drove Mom and me to school in his old beat-up car and then brought both of us back home.

The principal wanted my mom to get me to curtail my protesting activities and speech giving. He wanted to give me a three-day suspension, but mom persuaded him otherwise. Mom was respectful and dignified before the principal, but she was clearly not afraid, and I wasn't afraid either. After that, a fragile truce formed between the principal and me.

Mom never did try to stop me from protesting. We had been in the city for four years or so, and she had to work long, hard days cleaning houses. I don't know if she had the capacity to curtail my activities. I don't know where my father stood on my attitude. He was back on the plantation and not in my life.

Before they call, I will answer;
while they are yet speaking, I will hear. (Isaiah 65:24)

✤ God's Grace

Everyone wants to be listened to and heard. What you have to say is important. It is also critical that you learn to listen to others, because what they have to say can be important as well. As you listen to others, your viewpoint might change. But even if it doesn't, you might come to understand why they feel the way they do.

Listening to others is also a great way to show them that they are valuable. Pope Francis calls this an "apostolate of listening." He says,

Listening is the first step in dialoguing, and I think this is a problem which we must resolve. One of the worst ailments of our time is the poor level of listening skills. As if our ears were blocked. (Homily, March 12, 2017)

By listening closely to others, you can discover what each person around you needs in order to feel respected and loved.

How are your listening skills? Do you speak first in a challenging situation, rushing in with your own idea? Or do you listen first in order to really hear what the other person thinks and feels? Consider what a difference it would have made to me—to all black people in similar situations—if that principal had had "ears to hear" (Matthew 11:15).

What difference could you make in someone's life today if you really listened with the intention of understanding? Commit yourself to an apostolate of listening, and ask the Holy Spirit to help you "unblock" your ears so that you can be truly present, in God's name, to others.

CHAPTER FOURTEEN

HARASSMENT

With all my mom had to do, it was just too tough to keep up with our large family. During that time, we moved to a house on Atlanta Street that butted up against the levee of the Mississippi River, near a bar called Charlie's Blue Room. It was a dangerous place. For the first time in my life, I saw a guy with a needle hanging out of his arm. I knew that guy's brother.

I never went into Charlie's Blue Room. I was afraid to even walk by there. But I had to stand beside it every morning to get the bus.

I tried to join the Black Panther Party in New Orleans. I hadn't softened in my attitude: I still figured we should be killing the whites who were unfair to blacks, and I wanted to be the one in charge of that. Thanks to God's amazing grace, I couldn't come up with enough money for a bus ticket so that I could go find this group operating in New Orleans.

The Jefferson Parish police regularly stopped me for no other reason except that I was walking through a white neighborhood after basketball practice. I had no choice. In order to catch the bus home, my friends and I had to walk through the white neighborhood where our school was. Police officers would stop and search us and ask us what we were doing there, though it was obvious we were on our way home from school. They made us put our hands on the car and spread our legs like criminals. It was ongoing general harassment, but avoiding the police was like trying to dodge those little brown snakes back in Hollybrook.

And it wasn't only the police who harassed us. When we had to catch the bus home from basketball practice, we could never stand right at the bus stop in the white neighborhood, because if we stood there, some of the young white guys would throw bottles and other things at us from the windows of their cars. So we'd wait nearby, and as the bus got closer, we'd run up to it, hoping that the bus would wait so that we could catch our ride to our neighborhood. And harassment didn't stop once we got to our own neighborhood. The police often searched and questioned us even there.

A life of skirting around whites and being treated like a criminal caused the hatred inside me to grow. It was hard to suppress those feelings that had been festering for such a long time. But then something unexpected happened, and my thinking took a turn. Slowly things began to change.

> The LORD is a stronghold for the oppressed,
>   a stronghold in times of trouble. (Psalm 9:10)

✿ God's Grace

Living in a community where oppression seems to come from all sides, a place that leaves a person in constant fear and anxiety, takes a toll. Sometimes our enemies appear to multiply. Everything around us seems to aggravate us, and nothing seems to go our way. I experienced this as a result of racial prejudice, but it can happen to anyone caught up in a deeply stressful situation.

Where can we turn to find peace and rest? When we walk with the Lord, even when we are faced with enemies, the Lord reminds us, as he did King David, that even though we walk in the shadow of death, he is with us (see Psalm 23). By his power and grace, he will set the table before us in the presence of our foes.

God offers us peace beyond our understanding (see Philippians 4:7). Do you take him up on that offer? Do you ask him to help you settle into that peace? We know that he will help us, because the Bible says,

> The LORD withholds no good thing
>> from those who walk without reproach. (Psalm 84:12)

This passage is meant for you and for all those in stressful times who turn to the Lord for comfort and strength. Begin today to open your heart to the peace that God offers you. He will not withhold it. You might have to ask more than once, and you might have to train yourself to let go of your fear or anxiety or anger, but know that God will not fail to answer your prayer.

> For God will hide me in his shelter
>> in time of trouble,
> He will conceal me in the cover of his tent;
>> and set me high upon a rock. (Psalm 27:5)

CHAPTER FIFTEEN

THANKSGIVING

On Thanksgiving Day, my whole family was together except for A. C. and my dad. We had little to eat, but we were happy. We had indoor plumbing, with a toilet that flushed most of the time, and one of those party-line black rotary-dial phones. Our house was small, cramped, and in need of repair, but we were together.

We didn't have any food on this Thanksgiving Day except for some greens. Then, as my mother started to prepare the greens, there was a knock at the door. No one moved for several seconds. It felt as if time had stopped. Finally, somebody opened the door, to reveal a white woman holding a bag of groceries. She had red hair and manicured fingernails.

My mother was never a racist, but she always said we had to be careful around white people. And so we all just stood there looking at each other. I wondered about the white woman's motives. I wondered if she was going to turn us over to the landlord. We were always concerned that the landlord would demand more rent if he knew that ten people were living in a house that was meant for four or five. Why did she come on Thanksgiving Day?

One of my brothers went to the door and received the bag. We couldn't believe it! The bag was full of bread, all kinds of stuffing, fresh duck, and smoked oysters in a can. We had never tasted canned oysters, which we assumed had to be something very special. We couldn't afford oysters, in the can or otherwise. Clearly, the woman had just been to the grocery store, purchased these groceries, and brought them to our house.

Nobody knew who this woman was. It had been our understanding that when white people knocked on the door, it was the police, a gas leak, a fireman, a bill collector, or just plain trouble. Out of all the poor people in our neighborhood, however, somebody with a bag of groceries was on our doorstep. To us she seemed like an angel of mercy. She gave us the groceries with a warm smile, and then suddenly she was gone.

There I stood, a young angry black man with a big Afro and a mean look on my face. But now I was confounded. This knock on the door by a mysterious woman was the first sign that God's amazing grace was rushing in to help me overcome the power of race in my life. Looking back, I realize that this woman was on an assignment from God. As she came to my family, God's grace came into my life through her unforeseen act of kindness.

To this day, during Thanksgiving we inevitably speak of this unknown woman, and we all agree that she was a messenger from God, an angel doing God's bidding. This woman with fiery red hair was one of the arrows in the quiver of the Lord, and she allowed herself to be used by him. I couldn't hate her. Her skin color marked her as an enemy, but for no reason, she brought us much-needed food.

My mom and sisters cooked up a great meal, and we all ate until we were filled. It was a memorable day, never to be forgotten by me and my whole family.

Sometimes it only takes one act of kindness in the name of Jesus to set off a chain reaction of kindness in others. The woman who gave us food for Thanksgiving was supplying not only food for a meal but food for thought. I began to see that not all people with white skin were bad. Jesus had given me the opportunity to make a change in my thought process, and I took it.

My God will fully supply whatever you need, in accord with his glorious riches in Christ Jesus. (Philippians 4:19)

God's Grace

Personally, I truly believe that God sends angels disguised as people into our lives, and we don't recognize them for what they are. The Catholic Church says, "The existence of the spiritual, non-corporeal beings that Sacred Scripture usually calls 'angels' is a truth of faith. The witness of Scripture is as clear as the unanimity of Tradition" (*CCC*, 328).

Even more, the angels "serve [God's] saving plans for other creatures" and "protect every human being" (*CCC*, 350, 352). All I can say is that that woman, whoever she was, brought more than groceries into my life; she brought the beginning of healing.

We are not angels, but we can bring healing to others as well. You think, for example, that your little acts of kindness or your warm smile means nothing, but often such actions have the power to soften a hard heart or to redirect a young mind.

As you go about your day, notice the people who smile at you, and say a prayer of thanksgiving for them and their kind deed. Try to smile kindly at others as well, and ask God to bless them. That smile or any small courtesy you extend could start a chain reaction of healing and the opening of a person's heart to God.

CHAPTER SIXTEEN

CHANGE

I found myself slowly giving whites the benefit of the doubt, mainly because of that white woman who had extended grace to our family during Thanksgiving. I couldn't say that my hatred of whites had totally dissipated, but after the scene at our house with the groceries and our surprise visitor, it was starting to fade.

And there was another incident. To my surprise, when I was a junior in high school, the class elected me as their class representative. Also, some of the white students came to me privately and told me that they agreed with me, even if they didn't join in the protests.

Because I excelled at basketball, I received several scholarship offers. I accepted the one to McNeese State University in Lake Charles, Louisiana. I knew I was fortunate to have a way to get a college education.

My two younger brothers, Jimmy and Bobby, worked every day after school cutting people's grass and cleaning around their houses to help me as well as they could while I was in college. My older brother James began sending me five or ten dollars in the mail. I think he was proud of me when I got the basketball scholarship. James supported me in every way—he was always very good to me and generous with his money. Even though I had the scholarship, I still needed things like snacks, toothpaste, and miscellaneous items.

During the first year of college, I found myself maturing and calming down. For the first time, I began to slip more deeply into studies and further away from radical ideas. I made the dean's list several times, and overall, I did well in college.

He will wipe every tear from their eyes. (Revelation 21:4)

🌺 God's Grace

Just as it helps to be encouraged, it also helps others to be encouraged by you. When you offer encouragement to other people, you are beginning a culture of encouragement. Others will offer encouragement in return.

Be the first to take this step. Offer someone sincere encouragement about his schoolwork or her athletic ability, or choose someone at the office or church to encourage. Encourage this person consistently. You can even do it for a set period of time, as sort of an experiment, if you want to be convinced of the importance of being an encourager.

Encouragement can take many forms: an e-mail letting someone know how much he has meant to you, a phone call sharing your appreciation for hard work completed, a conversation encouraging someone to continue with a Bible study, or an expression of interest in something that is important to that person. Watch the results. The person will begin to stand up straighter, smile, be more self-confident, and perhaps begin to encourage others.

As the culture of encouragement begins to take hold, negative, unhelpful criticism will decline. Try to express yourself in a positive way, and consider encouraging someone today!

CHAPTER SEVENTEEN

A CALL

During summer break from college, I came home for a visit and helped my brothers with their grass mowing and cleaning jobs. People still yelled racial slurs at us as we waited for the bus to take us home from work, and young white guys still threw glass bottles at us from their passing cars while we stood on Metairie Road. Every day that we made it home without being called the "n word" or being injured was a good day.

One day an older white couple across the street from where I worked gave me some used plates and other utensils to bring home. They were impressed by the good job I had done on their neighbor's yard and asked me to cut their lawn too. I had to walk through their white neighborhood to catch the bus, so they gave me a note explaining that they had given me these things. They knew that any young black man walking through a neighborhood near Metairie Road carrying household items would certainly be stopped by the police and arrested as a thief.

I had a nervous feeling in my stomach all the way home. The reality of the social situation we found ourselves in was as daunting as ever.

To escape the demoralizing constraints one afternoon, my brothers and I decided to go fishing near the Gulf of Mexico. We caught the ferryboat to cross the Mississippi River, and while we were crossing, a man came up to me and said, "I saw you, and I see that God is doing something in your heart. God has been waiting for you to give your heart to him."

I was stunned! I didn't understand what he was saying or what was happening. I thought the whole thing was strange. I figured the guy was a religious fanatic, even though he didn't seem fanatical. He was calm and spoke very calmly to me. While he spoke, I just stood there trying to look casual, but as the ferryboat continued crossing the Mississippi, I leaned on the rail trying not to look bewildered. I was speechless.

I realize now that the man was simply riding back and forth waiting for people. He was a fisher of men! He was preaching the Word and inviting people to come to the Lord. The ferryboat was his pulpit, and I was one of the fish he was trying to catch. He did it with conviction but without emotional fervor—at least not on the outside.

That was the first time I was publicly evangelized. Somebody was actually witnessing to me about the Lord. In my heart, I felt that God was speaking through that man.

I never met him again; I have no idea who he was. I can see now that this was some kind of sovereign act of God. The man gave me a tip—a Holy Spirit tip—that God wanted to do something in me. It shook me to the core for many months.

After that day, I kept waiting for someone else to speak to me the way the man on the ferry had spoken to me. I was waiting for some follow-up person to tell me more. My heart was starting to open to the movement of God. I wanted to hear another word from God.

I contemplated, in my ignorance and lack of understanding, what the man had said: that God had been looking for me and wanted me to give my heart to him. I had no idea what that meant. I didn't tell my brothers. I didn't tell anybody. I wasn't even sure what in the world was going on inside me.

I felt an unmistakable void inside for the first time, and I also felt that it was somehow connected to the message that the man on the ferry had given me. Looking back now, I can see how this encounter (and later, many similar encounters) brought me to a place where my heart was beginning to be open to the action of the Holy Spirit.

In all circumstances give thanks, for this is the will of God for you in Christ Jesus. (1 Thessalonians 5:18)

🌺 God's Grace

Today I am so grateful for that man, who took seriously his divine call to plant seeds of faith and spoke to me about God. He wasn't just being a nice guy; he was intentional and all about the mission God had given him. Even though I can't thank him personally, I've learned that expressing thanks is another essential piece to a healthy spiritual life. God has given us so much—some things that we're aware of and some things yet to come—and it is imperative that we take the time to give thanks. Conveying our thanks to God helps us to keep him first in our thoughts and recognize that we owe everything to him.

As you begin to thank God for the individual things that he has blessed you with and for his movement in your life, you will begin to see how much he has done for you. This helps you grow in your faith. You see what God has already done, and you begin to trust more and more that he will continue to be a part of your life.

Every morning as you prepare for your day, list three things for which you are thankful that week. Start big, and then work your way to the individual things. For example, one morning you might thank God for the fact that you are alive, for the sunshiny day, and for the gift of your family. As you become more familiar with this practice, you may find yourself thanking God for your ability to get so much done at work the day before, for healing the soreness in your back, or for helping you to have patience with your children that week.

God wants to be a part of your life. Thanking God is just one way to invite him in more fully.

Chapter Eighteen

Marriage

After my first two years of college, I switched schools and attended Nicholls State University in Thibodaux, Louisiana. I was a typical college student, searching for my place in life. Nicholls was only about two hours away from where my brother James lived, and he would drive his old car up to get me during the breaks and bring me home.

After all the other boys had left home, James put off getting married and stayed to support my mother at the house. He delayed his own life and took care of Mom and the house out of his own means. The house was still a gathering place, but it was all done with James' work and finances.

At Nicholls I met, dated, and married a woman who was from a different cultural and ethnic background. She was an artist, and our classes happened to be in the same building. My new wife and I moved to Boulder so that I could begin studying at the University of Colorado. I was intent on getting a doctorate in psychology.

I don't know why I chose psychology—probably because somebody described it to me as the "helping profession." I liked the idea of helping people and saw psychology as a way to do that. I thought I might teach psychology at the college level or be a clinical psychologist. I mainly wanted to teach.

I graduated with a bachelor of arts degree in psychology from Nicholls and began a master's program there before moving to Boulder. But after a short time in Boulder, I decided that, as a married man, I needed to enter the workforce. I still thought that at some point, I'd go back and try to get my doctorate, however. I loved the world of education, teaching, and learning. I thoroughly enjoyed college and the engagement with the professors and the other students.

I was living free from the poverty that I had always known. I had a job and a good car. We were a young couple just getting started, and we had a good life.

> *Before they call, I will answer;*
> *while they are yet speaking, I will hear. (Isaiah 65:24)*

✹ God's Grace

You have natural gifts and talents that God gave to you at birth. There are spiritual gifts that God has given to you as well. Learning what your gifts and talents are—both natural and spiritual—is an important step in your spiritual journey. Using your gifts will help you develop them, just as an athlete who practices grows stronger and more confident. As you grow in your gifts, you will be able to find your place in the body of Christ.

A house is not built of only one piece of wood; it takes many. Together Christians make up the house of God—the body of Christ, the Church. You cannot stand alone; we need each other. We need every gift, and we need a variety of people with those gifts to help build the kingdom of God. As the First Letter to the Corinthians explains, we are all different parts of the same body, and we are all needed (see 1 Corinthians 12:4-26). If one person is a "foot" and they decide to be an "eye," then who will be the foot? And what will the one who was supposed to be an eye do?

We are all gifted with different sets of gifts, and they are all valuable in the body of Christ. Finding your gifts, using them wisely, and growing in them are ways for you to help build the kingdom of God.

✹

CHAPTER NINETEEN

QUEST FOR GOD

My wife and I moved to a suburb of New Orleans. After about three years, I was progressing with the company that I was working for, and they offered me a manager's job in Lake Charles, Louisiana. We moved there and rented a house.

I had more money and a better job than anybody in my family at that time. In fact, I was the first person in my family to get a college degree and have a professional job. My wife and I had money to buy extra items, like seafood, as well as our first new car. But we didn't like living in the Lake Charles area, and after a couple of years, we decided to move.

We bought a quaint old house in Ponchatoula, less than an hour outside of New Orleans. We had good credit, owned our own home, and had two beautiful children, but I had a nagging feeling of sadness inside of me. I had more time with my extended family, since we now lived closer to them, but my wife and I were mostly on our own, living our lives without God—like most of the people with whom we were acquainted. We seldom went to church, even though my wife had been a Catholic her whole life.

I was feeling as if there had to be more to life. The emptiness I felt led me to speculate about whether my father's absence had anything to do with my sadness. My dad wasn't in my life from junior high school through my college years. He never saw me play basketball. He didn't know that I got the scholastic award on my team as a senior in college; he wasn't there. He never knew that I was on the dean's list. These sad facts and his continuing absence in my life certainly added to the unhappiness and emptiness that I was experiencing.

I don't know what fully sparked it, but I began my quest for God. I didn't recognize what was going on, but I know now that it was the Holy Spirit at work. God was missing in my life. At twenty-five years of age, I was having my own adult "mourning bench" experience.

I read the Bible from front to back without gaining any understanding. I was simply searching, and my wife tried to help. Part of my search involved listening to religious programs on the radio every day as I drove to and from work. I'd listen to anything that had a religious connotation. I was looking for something to clear up the questions swirling around in my mind.

In the throes of my search, I still felt a sorrow. I had a house and a car, and I was not only doing well in my job but advancing. Yet I was still sad. I couldn't figure out where this emptiness was coming from.

We lived about thirty-five minutes away from my family in Kenner, but our lifestyle was so different from the way the rest of my family lived that we felt somewhat alone. Still, I often drove down to meet my brothers to go fishing. I came to realize that I was not as strong on the race issue as I had once been. My mind had turned to deeper things.

I wanted to know about the Bible and about God. All I could do was read the Bible, but I read it the way you read a novel, so maybe that's why I didn't grow in understanding. As time went on, however, I could see that I retained quite a bit more than I thought. And yet, I still didn't know exactly what I was searching for, except maybe for the meaning of *my* life.

I don't know if my college psychology classes played a role in my quest for something deeper; they may have. I believe, however, that it was a sovereign move of God—a heart searching for God and God searching for a heart that wanted to receive him. I know now that this is called "grace," which is unmerited favor given from God through many sources, including the sacraments, circumstances, and people.

> *Then the LORD will guide you always*
> *and satisfy your thirst in parched places,*
> *will give strength to your bones*
> *And you shall be like a watered garden,*
> *like a flowing spring whose waters never fail. (Isaiah 58:11)*

God's Grace

It always helps to have someone to talk with when we're wrestling with big issues. At this point in my search for meaning, I was more or less on my own. I think my isolation fed my sadness and depression. I think the same is true for a lot of people.

Basically, I was living to accumulate "stuff." I got the stuff, but I was still sad and depressed. Sometimes these feelings are openings through which God reaches out to us, inviting us to get to know him and his love. I could have just continued on the path I was on, with the goal of getting *more* stuff, but God was using the sadness to speak to my heart.

Is God calling you to look beyond the acquisition of more goods to embrace a higher calling in him? Who can you talk with about the direction of your life and about what God might be asking of you? What would it take for you to invite the Holy Spirit into your life or more deeply into your life?

No matter where you are on your spiritual journey, God has much more for you. Ask him to take your hand and lead you higher, deeper, and further into his plan and his love for you.

CHAPTER TWENTY

CATECHESIS

My neighbor at that time happened to be a salesman. One day he came over to my house and told me that he thought I could be a good salesman.

"I don't have time to sell at your company," I told him. "I have to get my life right with God." It was like the words gushed out on their own. I couldn't believe they came from me.

Today I know that when a searching heart is open, we, as the body of Christ, should be ready to share our faith. My heart was open, but up to that point, nobody had presented Jesus Christ as the Son of the living God to me in any detail.

My wife called a Catholic deacon who was a friend of hers, who later became a dear friend of mine and still is. The deacon came over, shared information about the Catholic faith with me, and began to teach me about the Catholic Church. He patiently answered my many questions.

When the deacon and I first met, I admit I was a bit confrontational. I didn't know this man. I didn't realize the training he and all Catholic deacons had to go through to be deacons or even that the diaconate was an ordained ministry. Consequently, at our first few encounters, he didn't have much stature in my eyes.

As time passed, however, the thing that impressed me about him was that he had been a deacon for many years and was able to give me some historical perspective on what it was like to be a black Catholic Christian. For example, he remembered having to sit in the back of the church. I could relate to this man and many of the struggles that he had to go through as a black man, except that his struggles also took place in the Church. He could identify with the difficulty of being black in a Church that is mostly white. (Today the African-American Catholic population makes up about 3 percent of the 70 million Catholics in the United States.)

This man was also a skilled minister. He had been trained by the Benedictines and knew the liturgy, played the keyboard and piano, and could sing. He was the first black deacon that I met.

My first few questions to him were "*Why do Catholics eat flesh and drink blood?*" and "*What is with all the kneeling and standing and sitting—why can't you just pray?*"

Looking back, I realize that he was very patient and kind with me. He was ready to answer all my questions—there was no hesitation in his answers or his testimony to me. My catechesis with him would last two years. As a result, I continued my journey of faith.

I will instruct you and show you the way you should walk,
give you counsel with my eye upon you. (Psalm 32:8)

❦ God's Grace

Scripture teaches us that we should desire "meat, not milk" (see 1 Corinthians 3:2). We need to move beyond our initial grasp of the faith and grow into deeper understanding. Spending time with one Scripture passage to digest what it means can help us do that.

From time to time, everyone comes across a Scripture passage that causes them to pause and think, *I understand this Scripture on one level, but I know that this passage is important, and I'm just not getting it all*. Or something similar.

When you come across a Scripture passage like this, deal with it by praying about it and studying it. (The footnotes in many Catholic Bibles are good places to start.) Ask the Holy Spirit to enlighten you, to help you see how the passage should affect your life in a real and personal way. This may take days, weeks, or even months. Don't give up. Don't stop studying, praying for revelation, or "chewing" on it.

When you begin to understand the passage, stay with it until you discern that you have everything that God wants to give you *at this time*. Years from now, you may find that God wants to teach you something different about that same Scripture passage. It doesn't mean that you "missed" something earlier. God is gentle, and he only gives you what you can handle at the time.

Overall, remember that every Scripture is both "milk" and "solid food" (1 Corinthians 3:2). Every Scripture offers us an encounter with the Word made flesh, Jesus Christ. As you "chew" over a Scripture and think about it, you are reflecting on the Lord and your relationship with him.

CHAPTER TWENTY-ONE

A RETREAT

Even after some months of talking with the deacon, I was not quite fully on board with *the Catholic thing*. As a result, when my wife wanted me to go on a retreat, there were intense negotiations. I thought we were just going to a meeting. I had never been on a retreat in my life, especially one involving religion where you had to go away overnight. I did *not* want to go.

But I went to this event, which was held at a retreat center in the Northshore area of New Orleans. I told my wife that my stomach was upset, and I would probably only stay for one day.

A lady named Hattie came to babysit for our children while we were gone. Hattie was a strong young black woman who had several children of her own. We felt safe leaving the kids with her. She was a good cook, a good housekeeper, and a great woman of God. She loved our children.

So I had no excuses. God had boxed me in.

On the retreat, I mainly tried to stay out of the way. I thought the whole thing was very weird. People were praying in a strange way that I now know is one of the gifts of the Holy Spirit, the gift of tongues. Everybody seemed to be beaming, very happy, kind of calm and peaceful. My wife seemed very happy too.

I found myself lost at this retreat and wanting to avoid people. I tried to hang back and just be invisible, but out of nowhere, this short, smiling, blond woman named Sue came right up to me. (Sue would later become my godmother.) With her piercing eyes, she looked me in the eye.

Sue could somehow see things. She knew things about me before I said a word. She had an inner brightness of spirit about her and presented herself like a faith-filled child. The fact that she was white didn't bother me, but I was unnerved by the uncanny way she could sense that my heart was troubled. "How are you doing?" she asked me.

I said, "Alright."

"It doesn't look like you are doing alright." And then she said, "God loves you, Larry."

I thought, *I don't even know her; she just met me; how does she know my name?* For no apparent reason, I immediately began to cry, and I could not stop. I had no idea why. I didn't know what was happening to me.

Sue said those three simple words that I will never forget: "God loves you." I believe that was the first time anybody had ever said those words to me.

> For the LORD gives wisdom,
>   from his mouth come knowledge and understanding.
> (Proverbs 2:6)

❀ God's Grace

When you go away on a retreat, you go to a specific place—usually quiet and away from the distractions of this world—and stay for a length of time, to be with God and to consider spiritual matters. Some of these are group retreats that have a set theme. Some are individual or private retreats, where you can usually speak periodically with a spiritual director or a priest.

For some people, the hardest part of a retreat is being away from the distractions of the world—no cell phones, computers, games,

TV, or magazines. Once people get over that culture shock, they tend to relax and just go with it.

It isn't necessary to go away to a retreat house in order to have a successful retreat. Also, the length of a retreat differs according to the needs of the person. For some people, a half-day retreat can be just as fulfilling as a weeklong retreat for someone else. For someone who has never taken a retreat, it can help to start with short one- or two-hour retreats and then, over time, work up to longer retreats as needed.

For those who are trying to make a big decision or discern something important—if you should get married, for example, or which college you should go to or whether to have a child or if you should take a missionary trip—a longer retreat may be necessary.

For most of us, it is good to get away every few months for at least half a day (four hours or so), to offer God our undivided attention. This allows us to step away from everyday life and take a look at the big picture. If you take up this practice, you'll find not only a time of refreshment but also a time when you can hear from the Lord about your life.

CHAPTER TWENTY-TWO

SCRIPTURE AND THE EUCHARIST

On that retreat, I got hold of a Bible, and the first Scripture I read that meant anything to me was in the Gospel of John: "Whoever eats my flesh and drinks my blood has eternal life, and I will raise him on the last day" (John 6:54).

At that moment, I knew that the Eucharist was real. I knew this Church was where I needed to be. I knew that I was going to become a Catholic.

I had been nothing as far as faith was concerned. I had been a wanderer. I was a lost soul. Now I was found. The eyes of my understanding were being enlightened, and I was beginning to know what the Letter to the Ephesians refers to as "the hope" of his calling:

May the eyes of [your] hearts be enlightened, that you may know what is the hope that belongs to his call, what are the riches of glory in his inheritance among the holy ones. (Ephesians 1:18)

I was finally seeing with eyes of faith, as if my eyes were suddenly opened.

At Mass during that retreat, I saw the host lifted up, and I knew that what the priest proclaims at this point in the Mass is true: "Behold the Lamb of God, behold him who takes away the sins of the world. Blessed are those called to the supper of the Lamb." This was Jesus Christ being praised and lifted up. This was Communion! This sacrifice was the same one that Jesus offered at Calvary.

"Unless you eat the flesh of the Son of Man and drink his blood, you do not have life within you. Whoever eats my flesh and drinks my blood has eternal life, and I will raise him on the last day" (John 6:53-54). I was caught up in those words.

Again, at that point I knew that I was supposed to become a Catholic. I don't know how I knew; I just knew. There is a knowing by the Spirit, and I knew that God had called me home to the Catholic Church, even though I didn't know much about it. This was what I wanted.

A great thirst welled up in me for the Eucharist, the Body and Blood, Soul and Divinity of Jesus Christ. I was exuberant! I felt caught up in something mystical. My heart was overjoyed, feeling the love of God—his light, his glory, his peace, and his joy surrounding me. I still had a long way to go, but God, by his sovereign will and by his grace, was sweeping me up into something.

My wife was very happy for me. I had once told her that I would never become a Catholic. I told her she could raise the children Catholic, but "Catholics are just too weird for me." I could not get over the fact that Catholics eat flesh and drink blood. Cannibalism is evil, or illegal, or something! It had to be.

Now I was seeing Catholics go to Holy Communion and get a little piece of bread and drink from a common cup. In an instant, all doubt was erased. This truly was the Lamb of God; this was the Lord! That was one of the life-changing moments in my life.

The Holy Spirit was moving in my heart and in my life. He was leading me and revealing truth to me, but he was also revealing what was not truth. When Jesus called the disciples, he told them, "I am the way and the truth and the life" (John 14:6). The Holy Spirit had protected me, and thanks be to God, my wife had called the deacon to teach me the faith and help me understand the Catholic Church.

I finally grasped, in my childlike faith, that I could be forgiven and that God had covered my sin with his own blood. I was being ushered into what I had always thought of as "the white man's Church," but I was learning that it is God's Church, and race does not matter to God.

> *Then Peter proceeded to speak and said, "In truth, I see that God shows no partiality." (Act 10:34)*

I was becoming a Catholic. I started going to some of the prayer meetings, where people were praying in the Spirit (praying in tongues) and laying hands on people in prayer. It was an awesome time.

> *The grass withers, the flower wilts, but the word of our God stands forever. (Isaiah 40:8)*

☘ God's Grace

As I have noted here and there, reading and studying the Word of God are essential if you want to grow in your faith. Every time you open your Bible is a time God can and will speak to you. Even if you read the same passage every day for a week, that Scripture can speak to you in a different way every time. The Bible is the living Word of God.

Bible study cannot be stressed enough. In order to follow God's will, you must know God's will. St. Jerome said it best: "Ignorance of Scripture is ignorance of Christ" (*Commentary on Isaiah*). If you want to get to know your Lord and Savior better, then you must read about him and his life, study what he said and did, and understand how the Old Testament and all the prophets relate to the New Testament. Yes, the Christian faith is to be experienced, but you must grow in your knowledge of the faith in order to pass on the truth. If you confess that you believe in Jesus, the Christ and Son of God, then it is important that you know who he is.

Reading the Bible and partaking of the Eucharist go hand in hand: the Bible leads you to the Eucharist, and the Eucharist opens up your understanding of the Bible. Even the Mass is structured so that the reading of the Scriptures leads into the Eucharist. Ask the Lord, when you receive Holy Communion, to open the meaning of the Scriptures to you. You will find, as you do this over time, that the Holy Spirit will lead you into new and deeper understanding.

CHAPTER TWENTY-THREE

MERCY

I was on my journey toward the Catholic Church and toward becoming a Christian, but I wanted to understand what was going to happen with all my sins. One day I heard a speaker tell a story that helped me in this regard.

In the 1700s, there was a great Indian tribe, blessed in every regard. The chief was a strong leader whose word was the law. Everything was going fine, and the tribe's people were thriving and doing well. They never had any problems. Their enemies didn't bother them because they were strong, with a strong leader.

But then a problem arose: someone was stealing. The chief said, "When we find that man, we'll give him fifty lashes at the hand of the taskmaster." But the stealing continued.

Then the chief spoke again: "When we find the thief, we will give him one hundred lashes at the hand of the taskmaster." One hundred lashes would kill most men!

One day they found the thief. It was the mother of the chief. A great hush fell over the people and they asked, "Is he going to satisfy his law?" Because when the chief spoke, his word became the law. "Will he satisfy his law, or will he satisfy his love?"

The chief loved his mother very much, but when the day for the punishment came, they brought her into the middle of the compound. She was a small, frail woman. They ripped her clothes from her, exposing her back, and bound her hands and feet.

Again a hush came over the people. Everyone wondered if the chief would satisfy his law at the expense of his love.

The chief raised his hand, and the taskmaster, muscles bulging, came forth with a huge whip in his hand, certain to kill the woman. The chief raised his hand and said, "Let the punishment begin." The people could not believe it; the chief was going to satisfy his law at the expense of his love.

The taskmaster drew back to deliver the first blow, and then the chief raised his hand again. Everybody gasped and said, "Oh, he's going to satisfy his love at the expense of his law." But then the chief took off his robe and headdress and handed them to the attendant, exposing his own strong back. He went over to where his mother was bound hand and foot, stretched out his arms, and covered his mother with his own body. "Let the punishment continue," he said. In that way he satisfied his law and his love.

The speaker who told the story went on to explain that Jesus Christ has covered our sins, because Scripture says, in the Letter to the Romans, "The wages of sin is death" (Romans 6:23).

I knew that I was a sinner. But Jesus had covered me with his body and his own blood. In my heart, I knew he was saying, "Father, see my body; see my blood, shed at Calvary for Larry. Don't count his sin against him."

With this new understanding, a passage in the Book of Isaiah became clear to me:

> But he was pierced for our sins,
>   crushed for our iniquity.
> He bore the punishment that makes us whole,
>   by his wounds we were healed. (Isaiah 53:5).

After that, more of the Scriptures began to make sense. Psalm 103 spoke to me directly: "I've separated your sin as far as the east is from the west, and I remember it no more" (cf. verse 12).

All these things were becoming clearer to me and helping me understand what being a child of God means. That story about God's love and his law had a great influence on my life; it was the beginning of my building faith upon faith.

From afar the LORD appears:
With age-old love I have loved you;
so I have kept my mercy toward you. (Jeremiah 31:3)

✿ God's Grace

As the story of the Indian chief makes clear, God can bring great things from what is bad. He can redeem any situation.

But why do bad things happen? For various reasons, of course. Sometimes it's clear, and sometimes it's not; the bad thing just seems random. And sometimes you cannot understand why certain things happen to you versus someone else or no one at all. Even worse, when you see others getting something good, it can be hard to be happy for them and not upset for yourself.

People often choose to blame God when bad things happen; perhaps you do too. You might feel free to because. in the back of your mind, you know that God will still love you.

Over the next week, if something happens that upsets you, take it to God in prayer. It's okay to ask him questions, to seek his wisdom. Ask the Holy Spirit to guide you in your response to the situation. Ask for understanding. Even if perfect understanding doesn't come all at once, or ever, you may find that you understand better ways to pray about the situation.

Pray for good to come out of the incident. Pray that you can act in holiness and that you receive wisdom about how you should respond. Over time, as you do this, situations will lose their power to distress you as much. You will automatically go to God first and allow the Holy Spirit to guide you through all things.

CHAPTER TWENTY-FOUR

RCIA AND THE TRANSITION

Most people who are interested in becoming a Catholic go through a nine-month or so program known as the Rite of Christian Initiation of Adults (RCIA). As I've mentioned, I had one-on-one catechesis with the deacon for two years. He worked to answer all of my questions and to teach me the faith.

During this time, I went to many charismatic events throughout the Archdiocese of New Orleans and the surrounding areas. The charismatic community embraced me. There was so much joy in those events, and it was a great time of healing for me. I encountered many white people who were good and kind—great men and women of God! I began to go to Mass more regularly. During this time, God was healing me of my prejudices.

Attending Mass and going to these events would bring up more questions for me, but the deacon answered them all with patience, kindness, and confidence. (This taught me to value one-on-one evangelization.) My heart was very open to receiving the truth of the gospel. This truth is what I had been searching for. I learned that true evangelization has to be built on confidence in the gospel message.

I realize now, looking back, that the attention this deacon gave me during my catechesis filled something important that had been missing from my life: he was not only a brother; he was kind of a father to me. My respect for him grew during our time together, and I came to value his mentorship and friendship.

By God's grace, all these years later, I have been privileged to minister to him and his family as this man of God enters into advanced age.

As we begin to believe in God and believe God, our trust and faith will grow. This faith, this trust in God's presence and promises, is essential. Pope Francis told the young people at World Youth Day in Rio de Janeiro,

> *Faith accomplishes a revolution in us . . . ; it removes us from the center and puts God at the center; faith immerses us in his love and gives us security, strength, and hope. Seemingly, nothing has changed; yet, in the depths of our being, everything is different. (Homily, July 25, 2013)*

It's like that old gospel song: "Something on the inside is working on the outside. Oh, what a change in my life."

That's what was happening to me over the years, as I moved away from hatred of white people—something was working in me, on the inside. It was a progression toward faith and, finally, *in* faith.

With faith and trust, we learn to depend on God, to seek him and to tell him when we have needs, confident that God, in his mercy, will provide for us. God's provision may not come in the way we want or expect, but God does provide.

> *Then the LORD said to Moses: I am going to rain down bread from heaven for you. (Exodus 16:4a)*

Chapter Twenty-Five

Baptism

I came into the Catholic Church and became a Christian when I was twenty-seven. People often ask, "What did you convert from?"

I had never been baptized and had no previous formal religious affiliation. Although my mom had a Baptist background, I was not a Baptist and wasn't trained in the Baptist faith, except for the brief experience of church that I had as a young boy on the mourning bench. I can't say that I converted from anything. I like to say that I was just a regular heathen.

Now I felt as if I was caught up in something special. Everything was new. Everything Catholic was wonderful.

I shared with my brother James that I was going to become a Catholic. James, at this point, was not very churched himself, and neither were my other brothers. Later, as I've said, two of them would become ordained ministers.

Because the deacon had ministered at Our Lady of the Rosary Church on Bayou Lafourche, and because he was going to baptize me, we agreed that I would be baptized there. Yes, I was going down to the bayou to be baptized and to receive my first Holy Communion. I believe that I was one of the first black adults ever baptized there. *Lafourche* is French for "fork." The ironic symbolism dramatically describes my life-changing directional shift. This indeed was the fork in the road of my life.

The church was full. My mom and my brother George, who is now a Baptist minister, were there. Mom had previously said to the deacon, "Look, I understand Larry's going to be a Catholic, but I want to make sure that he goes under the water. I don't want just a sprinkling for my boy, even if he's going to be a Catholic."

To satisfy my mother, the deacon had a large tub of water brought in so that I could be immersed. The church even provided a white robe for me to wear when I received the sacrament of baptism.

I was emotional but calm. I was filled to overflowing. Everything was beautiful, and everything was set. I had been to prayer meetings on the bayou, and so I had met many of the people from the Catholic Charismatic Renewal community there. They all showed up to welcome me into the Church; it was a beautiful thing. I went down in the water with no fear. I was full of anticipation, filled up with God's love, his mercy, and his peace. I could not believe that I was being ushered into this great mystery of faith, of God, and of his people. My heart was spilling over with love.

I could hardly believe it, but all of the hate-filled thoughts that I had embraced in my past were now somehow gone. Calling white people "blue-eyed devils," wanting to take up arms and join the Black Panther Party—it was all gone. All of those feelings were swept away.

I carried a lot of pain from the indignity that I had suffered as a young man—that disappeared as well. All the pain of seeing my family struggle for so many years and the suffering we endured as the Jim Crow laws came to an end—gone. All of the humiliation in high school from a seemingly racist principal and teachers had vanished. My hatred of the people who threw the coke bottles, eggs, and garbage at me and my brothers while we waited for the bus after cutting their grass had been swept away.

I came out of the baptismal waters, and my mom, my brothers, and all of the white people there looked like they had the faces of angels. Everyone looked bright with light and beauty. Beaming. Wonderful. Peaceful.

Call to me, and I will answer you; I will tell you great things beyond the reach of your knowledge. (Jeremiah 33:3)

God's Grace

The seven sacraments of the Catholic Church are baptism, confirmation, Eucharist, reconciliation, anointing of the sick, holy orders, and matrimony. The *Catechism of the Catholic Church* teaches this:

> *The sacraments are efficacious signs of grace, instituted by Christ and entrusted to the Church, by which divine life is dispensed to us. The visible rites by which the sacraments are celebrated signify and make present the graces proper to each sacrament. (1131)*

When people go through the Rite of Christian Initiation and choose to be baptized, then they are saying that they are in agreement with what the Church teaches and that they will submit themselves to the Church's authority. A person joins the Church by receiving what is known as the sacraments of initiation: baptism, confirmation, and Eucharist.

As a Catholic, you can encourage others who are curious about the Catholic Church to go through the RCIA program. Even if they decide not to join the Church at that time, they will learn a lot and might come back in the future.

Do you know someone who is asking questions about the faith? Perhaps RCIA would be right for him or her.

Is God calling you to help your local parish with its RCIA program? Do you have the time and the calling to help others learn more about the Catholic faith? If so, consider speaking with the leadership in your parish to find out how you can help.

CHAPTER TWENTY-SIX

THE HOLY SPIRIT

After I was baptized, there was an anointing, a fire from the Holy Spirit that rested upon me. I had never experienced anything like that before. It was as if the dove of the Holy Spirit was over me, and he was a powerful and strong presence but also gentle. *Anointing* is the only word that I can use to describe it.

> *But you have the anointing that comes from the holy one, and you all have knowledge. (1 John 2:20)*

> *But the one who gives us security with you in Christ and who anointed us is God; he has also put his seal upon us and given the Spirit in our hearts as a first installment. (2 Corinthians 1:21-22)*

I can use that word *anointing* now to describe my state, but at the time, I certainly didn't know what it meant. I had heard about it but never experienced it.

The anointing was heavy and overpowering and remained with me for three or four days. I felt as if I had been swallowed up in the glory of God. There was a sense of God's holiness, a sense of his presence, a sense that I was now in God and God was now in me. I was aware of the presence of the Holy Spirit. I looked at the people I encountered in a new way; I had a new compassion in me. I think it had already started, but baptism, first Communion, and confirmation sealed it for me.

I was a new person. I was a new creation. I knew that's what Scripture says we are, but I could *feel* the sensations of change. I *felt* myself become a new person after I came out of the water and received Holy Communion for the first time. After I was confirmed in the Church, I was different. Altered. The old Larry was gone. I was a new being just as the Second Letter to the Corinthians says, and I *knew* it: "So whoever is in Christ is a new creation: the old things have passed away; behold, new things have come" (5:17). Old things truly had passed away and everything was genuinely new.

When I went back to work after that Thursday night service, Jimmy, a Catholic lawyer who worked for the same company as me, brought me a little gift and a card welcoming me to the Church. That meant so much to me. I kept that little card for at least seven or eight years after my baptism. It was a very important symbol of welcoming to me. Jimmy was the first person at my workplace to welcome me into the body of Christ. It was just an awesome time in my life.

A friend named Bob and I were co-workers, and Bob was caught up in my baptism. He was a cradle Catholic (a Catholic who was baptized as an infant and raised in the faith), and his faith was rekindled while experiencing my conversion process with me. Together we now went to the mall and talked to people about Jesus. We were on fire for God. There was an overflow of God's love, and I was experiencing an afterglow from my baptism.

I experienced this anointing of the Holy Spirit, this fire of God's love, when I received the sacraments, but many people experience it apart from the sacraments as well, when they are at prayer. Some people have this anointing when they receive what is known in the Charismatic Renewal as the "baptism in the Holy Spirit." This baptism in the Spirit takes place when an individual, in prayer, experiences a deeper surrender to God and invites the Holy Spirit to act more freely and powerfully in that person's life. (To learn more about the baptism in the Holy Spirit, go to the International Catholic Charismatic Renewal Services website, www.iccrs.org.)

Because my anointing came when I received the sacraments of baptism, confirmation, and the Eucharist for the first time, I didn't realize that I could experience this intimate presence of the Holy Spirit more than once. But as it is said, there is only one baptism but there are many "fillings." Once you are baptized, you receive the indwelling Holy Spirit permanently; however, a person can receive an infilling more than once.

I received the indwelling at baptism, but I was now experiencing the infilling and the overflow. I have experienced it many times since. It is not a hyperemotional experience, as many people think. It is vast, deep, wide, and weighty. It is the glory of God being made manifest or showing forth in a person's life, and he or she is aware of it. It is God's presence with us, in us, and around us.

Now the Lord is the Spirit, and where the Spirit of the Lord is, there is freedom. (2 Corinthians 3:17)

❧ God's Grace

The Holy Spirit is the third Person of the Holy Trinity, ever at our side if we ask him to be with us. He is "the 'Paraclete,' literally, 'he who is called to one's side,' . . . 'consoler,' . . . 'the Spirit of truth'" (*CCC*, 692). The *Catechism of the Catholic Church* teaches:

"Holy Spirit" is the proper name of the one whom we adore and glorify with the Father and the Son. The Church has

received this name from the Lord and professes it in the Baptism of her new children.

. . . On the other hand, "Spirit" and "Holy" are divine attributes common to the three divine persons. By joining the two terms, Scripture, liturgy, and theological language designate the inexpressible person of the Holy Spirit, without any possible equivocation with other uses of the terms "spirit" and "holy." (691)

Begin your day every day with prayer to the Holy Spirit, and ask him to lead and guide you. As you allow the Holy Spirit to lead your daily life, you may notice more divine encounters taking place. Those are unexpected moments that often seem impossible but that move God's kingdom forward, perhaps by giving you an opportunity to share your testimony or by putting you in the right place at the right time. Be sure to have your testimony ready, and whatever the circumstance, be sure to listen to the Holy Spirit.

CHAPTER TWENTY-SEVEN

LEARNING MORE

I left the insurance company I was working for and went to work for another insurance company that offered me a substantial raise. I couldn't refuse the offer. I worked for that company for almost four years in the Metairie area. Then that firm offered me a job at several places around the country, and I took the one in Seattle. I was regional manager over Alaska, Washington, Idaho, and Oregon.

It was a different situation in Seattle. My entire staff was white. Generally, people were very kind, and there wasn't any blatant racism such as I had experienced down South.

We prayed about whether we should move to Seattle, but in retrospect, I realize that God never really answered. He never said, "Go." I learned a valuable lesson. God didn't say "Go," but we went because he wasn't saying "No."

I had asked my deacon friend to pray with us. He said, "Well, you know he's going to tell you what to do." I didn't really understand what that meant, but I now know that when you ask God a question, you should wait for an answer.

Nevertheless, my career in Seattle went well. During the four-plus years that we were there, I worked with a great staff, earned good bonuses, and had a boat, two cars, and a large house in a great neighborhood. Our children attended a very good school.

We were actively involved in the Western Washington Catholic Charismatic Renewal, and we had friends in the community who readily accepted us. From my perspective, the move to Seattle was a success. My wife never fully adjusted to Seattle and the weather there, however, so we decided to move back to Louisiana.

Once back, we purchased the same house that we used to live in. One cannot recreate the past though; things are never the same as they once were. It was a difficult transition time for our family. We stayed in that house for less than a year and then moved to the area where I currently live.

I continued to learn about my faith from the deacon. He had now become more than just my teacher; he had become my friend.

We know that all things work for good for those who love God, who are called according to his purpose. (Romans 8:28)

❦ *God's Grace*

We have a tendency to want things *now*. Our culture constantly feeds into this tendency by offering us fast food, movies on demand, and other seemingly quick fixes to our needs. Prayer is different. When you pray and ask the Lord for help, you need to be prepared to wait patiently for an answer. Sometimes the answer may come quickly, and you can act on God's answer right away. At other times, the answer may take time.

The bottom line is that you need to learn to wait on the Lord. God's timing doesn't always align with your schedule, but he sees more than you do, and he knows what's best for you. If God is asking you to persevere in prayer right now but you are finding it hard to wait for his answer, ask yourself this: do I want to follow my will or God's will? Trust that he will lead you.

CHAPTER TWENTY-EIGHT

FORGIVENESS

As I began to allow the Holy Spirit to move in my life, God began to deal on a deeper level with many of the issues that had shaped my life. I wanted to confront my dad about his not taking care of our family, so I discovered where he lived—back in the country on the plantation—and went to see him. I asked him questions, but I chose my words carefully, trying not to be disrespectful. I didn't want to start a fight; I just wanted answers so that I could understand his absence and apparent lack of support. Maybe because I presented myself humbly to him, he was open to my questions and wanted to talk.

My dad pulled out a little box of money-order receipts that he had saved for fifteen years or more. I guess he knew that one day one of his children was going to ask him about these things once we were adults. He showed me that he had sent money orders of five dollars, ten dollars, or fifteen dollars every week to my mom to support our large family the best he could.

I was in tears. "Dad, I want to understand. Mom says that you didn't do enough for the family. Why didn't you send more? You knew we were struggling in the city. Why didn't you come and visit us?" I just wanted to know.

When God starts to move in your heart, you want to know the truth. Whether it is hard or ugly or painful, you just want truth, because "the truth will set you free" (John 8:32).

When I told my dad that we did a lot of fishing down near New Orleans, he asked me if I wanted to go fishing. The next thing I knew, we were fishing. For the first time in my life, I went fishing with my father. We went over the levee to the outlets from Lake Providence. He had a boat, a flatboat, in the back of his truck.

I was impressed that my dad was so strong at his age. He asked me if I could help him pull the boat out of the truck, and I nodded. He just laughed when I asked him if he had a pair of gloves. My dad was always a hard worker, and he was used to doing things with his hands.

"Don't worry about it, Son; I've got it." And he pulled the boat out of the truck by himself.

My dad treated me well, and we always shared a sense of reconciliation after my visit. I never regretted going and finding him and hearing his explanation. I cried with him. We cried with one another. I had never known him like this. I had a father! He was imperfect, but I was so happy to get to know him.

I hadn't been old enough to talk to my dad before he dropped out of my life; I was a child when we moved from the plantation. Children didn't speak to their parents with familiarity when I was growing up; that was considered disrespectful. But now I was back on the plantation, and I was talking to my dad. We talked like two men, not father and son.

We only caught two little fish, but it didn't matter because I was in the boat with my dad. I could tell by the way he cast and the way he steered the boat and studied the water that he was a good fisherman. There was an alligator swimming around in the area where we were, but my dad wasn't afraid. He told me, "That ol' alligator is not going to do anything."

I was a grown man, but even so, being with my dad made me feel safe. I wasn't worried. We didn't have any life jackets in the boat, I don't swim, and that water was deep, but I wasn't afraid. I was with my father.

That visit cleared up all of my questions in regard to my dad. He didn't act frustrated with me for asking so many personal questions. He didn't even seem to mind telling me things that I had no business asking. We talked all day, and then I stayed for a second day. It was a wonderful time.

Back on the plantation, working for the property owner, my father had given his whole life to that land. He just wore out from driving the tractors, working with the chemicals, and then having an injury on the job. He underwent back surgery as a result, and it turned out pretty bad. Health care was lacking, and he suffered for it.

I never went fishing with him again and never will, because he passed away years ago. Nevertheless, I have that memory solid in my mind. Dad and I bonded on that flatboat. I headed home with an overflowing heart of love for my dad.

Dad was buried on the plantation, but land can no longer hold him. He is now free because he died in faith.

Dad died in the summer of 2011. I had the privilege of sharing these words at his funeral:

There was a man named Job who had seven thousand sheep, three thousand camels, five hundred teams of oxen, and five hundred female donkeys. Job was rich! Upon his death, my dad had no sheep, no camels, no oxen, and no female donkeys. By all outward appearances, my dad was poor. Yet he died rich! He had thirteen sons, nine daughters [he had married and fathered a second family], scores of grandchildren and great-grandchildren. Through his loins came three ordained ministers—a Catholic deacon, a Baptist minister, and a Pentecostal minister—and two Baptist deacons. His faithful wife cared for him in his frailty toward the end of his life.

Three events about Dad stand out in my memory. One was when he came home early and caught us boys playing cards on top of the freezer. He didn't want us playing cards, and when he caught us, it was not a pretty sight, especially when he went to the tree to break off a limb (not a branch) to give out the punishment. I have many reasons to not be able to forget him in that moment.

The second memory was of the one and only time that I got to go fishing behind the levee with him. It was a father-son moment that I will treasure forever. Despite the fact that we only caught two small fish during that brief time together, we were able to catch something much bigger and more long lasting. I saw my dad as a father with his son.

The final memory was of my dad being baptized in the lake. He looked so serene as he approached and went down into the water! It was a great day for him and a great day for our family to see him come to faith in Jesus Christ. My mother was very happy for my dad, and she also attended his baptism, even though they had been estranged for many years.

Dad, you gave your whole life to the land, and now you will be buried on the land that you worked. Even though you will be buried there, neither the land nor its owners have a hold on you anymore. You are free now, Clifton/Bubba/Dad. Your struggle is over, and the Lord himself is extending his hand to you and saying, "Come now and enjoy all I have prepared for you. Come now, take up your rest in the new land."

If you forgive others their transgressions, your heavenly Father will forgive you. (Matthew 6:14)

Jesus often spoke about forgiveness. He even said that if we expect God to forgive us, then we must forgive others (see Matthew 6:14-15). It's a requirement! Without forgiveness, we can become bitter, and bitterness can lead to other sins. As Christians, we have to forgive everyone—not just other Christians, but everyone.

When you forgive someone, you acknowledge that he or she has hurt you, and you choose to pardon the person for that hurt. It doesn't mean that what that person did was right or alright to do; it just means that you are choosing not to hold that sin against them.

In the case of parents, it can be doubly devastating when they let a child down. Parents are supposed to take care of their children, but parents are human, and they make mistakes. The Scripture passage about noticing a splinter in someone else's eye while one has a wooden beam in his own is usually used, when teaching, to discuss hypocrisy, but it can also be used to talk about forgiveness.

Why do you notice the splinter in your brother's eye,
but do not perceive the wooden beam in your own eye?
(Matthew 7:3)

We want God to forgive the "wooden beam" in our eyes, but it is important that we forgive the "splinter" of someone else. Splinters can hurt, especially when they are from our family members. The only way to pull them out is by truly forgiving the person.

We all need to extend forgiveness at some point in our lives, usually fairly often. There is no way around this requirement if we want to be faithful and effective members of the Christian community.

🌸

CHAPTER TWENTY-NINE

THE WORD OF GOD

I continued to move deeper into the faith. About a year after I was baptized, someone asked me to teach a Bible study, and I did.

I love the Word of God—Old Testament and New Testament. I love studying the Word of God. I love everything about the Scriptures. I found it somewhat shocking that many Catholics didn't know much about the Bible. Grown people who had been faithful Catholics for many years didn't know anything about Scripture! Consequently, they seemed to know little about the promises of God, or about healing, or even believe that evil was real.

I was naturally inclined toward teaching, and it was not hard for me to begin to study the Bible in earnest rather than just read it. I was teaching the best psychology known to humanity—the love of God. The more I studied God's Word, the stronger my desire for the Word grew.

A priest friend who saw my desire gave me a concordance. (This was back before we had information available on the Internet.) I still have that concordance; it has helped me tremendously. "The word of God is living and effective," the Letter to the Hebrews says (4:12). I was experiencing that; the power of God's Word held me close to him and revealed to me his wonderfulness.

Eventually, my wife and I went to the pastor of the church we were attending and told him that we felt the Church needed more. He simply nodded and said, "Yeah, I know, so what are you going to do about it?"

I was dumbfounded. It wasn't the answer we were expecting, but we took up the challenge. The priest, my wife and I, and one of the nuns at Holy Rosary Dominican Retreat Center started a prayer group, the first charismatic prayer group there.

I also attended many meetings and charismatic Masses at the Center of Jesus the Lord, a parish in New Orleans led by Fr. Emile Lafranz. This Catholic charismatic parish, on the edge of the French Quarter, ministers in the powerful gifts of the Holy Spirit. At first, I thought that all Catholics were charismatic, but I quickly realized that although part of the Church was charismatic, other parts were not as open to the charismatic perspective.

Catholics who are involved in the Charismatic Renewal typically are very proactive about asking the Holy Spirit, given at baptism and again poured out during confirmation, to work in and through them. Charismatics are also open to the charismatic or spiritual gifts mentioned in St. Paul's First Letter to the Corinthians and other Scriptures: wisdom, knowledge, faith, gifts of healing, mighty deeds, prophecy, discernment of spirits, varieties of tongues, interpretation of tongues, and so forth. (There are certainly many Catholics who also experience the gifts of the Holy Spirit but wouldn't necessarily call themselves charismatic.)

Heaven and earth will pass away, but my words will not pass away. (Mark 13:31)

✤ God's Grace

We should regularly remind ourselves that, as Christians, we have a spirit not of timidity but of power (see 2 Timothy 1:7). This can make us uncomfortable because it means that we can't be couch potatoes, letting someone else do the work. We are called to step out in faith. As Pope Francis says,

My friends, Jesus is the Lord of risk, he is the Lord of the eternal "more." Jesus is not the Lord of comfort, security and ease. Following Jesus demands a good dose of courage, a readiness to trade in the sofa for a pair of walking shoes and to set out on new and uncharted paths. (Prayer Vigil, World Youth Day, July 30, 2016)

When the pastor asked my wife and me what we intended to do about the Church needing "more," we didn't expect to be challenged in that way. But it was a great reminder that we are all the Church, and we all need to step up and do our part.

Do you have a spirit of timidity? Or are you maybe just too comfortable and not looking for any more challenges? How is God asking you to step out to serve him?

We are all called to service until we go to be with him. What is he asking you to do, and how are you responding to his call?

CHAPTER THIRTY

ANSWERING THE CALL

I'm not sure how most men decide to become deacons, but I think many of us sense a calling prompted by the Holy Spirit. That's what happened to me. The Church helps the potential candidate discern if that calling is of the Lord. It's a two-pronged process.

First, the bishop appoints leaders to guide diaconate formation in his diocese, and these leaders help the candidate discern if the deaconate is the right ministry for him. This is the Holy Spirit at work within the hierarchy of the Church. Second, the Holy Spirit works in the heart and life of the potential diaconate candidate to help him discern his call.

I didn't know much about the diaconate when my godmother, Sue, gave me my first inkling that it might be for me. Of course, I knew some Catholic deacons, including my friend who catechized me, but I had no idea what their training involved. Still, I had seen him and other deacons in ministry, and I was struck by the way that these married men serve the Church. I wanted to serve the Church as well, but I didn't know if I would qualify.

I was thirty-one years old and had four children when I began to feel a call to be an ordained deacon in the Catholic Church. This was three or four years after coming into the Church. I looked into it but discovered that I was too young: a man had to be thirty-five before he could be accepted into the diaconate formation program. I was totally disappointed and didn't inquire again until I was thirty-nine.

I was accepted into the program, and I felt that I was following the prompting of the Holy Spirit to give my life to serve the Lord.

This was a full conversion for me. I wanted to follow God with my whole heart and to serve in any way that I could.

While I was in training for the diaconate, I was given permission to teach at a men's conference in Clarksdale, Mississippi, with a friend, the late Deacon Alex Jones. Deacon Jones was a black Catholic deacon from the Archdiocese of Detroit who had been a Pentecostal minister prior to coming into the Catholic Church. (When he converted, fifty members of his congregation also became Catholic.)

Someone drove us to the conference, and that freed us to focus and converse without thought for the road. As we rode along—two black men—we looked at one another and realized that twenty or thirty years ago, we would not have been traveling through Mississippi to preach at a white Catholic Church as the two principal teachers and speakers. It hit us: how good God is! Mississippi was once a desert for me, and now I was one of the people bringing the water of the Word into the desert, this place that had once filled me with fear.

Who can do something like that, except God?

Commit your way to the LORD;
trust in him and he will act. (Psalm 37:5)

✿ *God's Grace*

What does it mean to be "called"? When you are called by God into something, like a ministry, it means that you feel that the Lord is directing you to begin this new endeavor. Being called doesn't mean that the ministry will happen overnight; you still have to put in time, energy, and effort to train.

It helps to remember that, as the saying goes, God doesn't call the qualified, he qualifies the called. This is a key point to keep in mind if you think that God is calling you into a ministry but you are wondering how, when, where, who, or how much. Yes, you have to put in the time and make the commitment; however, it is by God's strength and with his resources that you reach your goals when you are called into ministry.

Another key point when accepting a call from God is that you have to be willing to accept the authority already in place—beginning with God, all the way through to the person who is currently leading the ministry that you want to join. Many people are willing to accept God's authority and even the Church's authority, but they struggle when it comes to accepting the authority of those who are currently in charge. God is a God of order, and showing that you can obey authority is important. Displaying that you have a teachable spirit is also essential to the success of your new calling.

Is God calling you to a new endeavor at this time? If so, what might that be? Are you open to putting in time, energy, and resources to succeed in your calling?

God also calls us to encourage others being called to serve in some kind of ministry. Do you encourage others to follow the promptings of the Holy Spirit?

CHAPTER THIRTY-ONE

CHANGE AND GROWTH

I was more than three years into the diaconate program and a year and a half from being ordained when my wife asked for a divorce. This was extremely difficult. I was in the desert. The only thing I had was God. I had my mom and siblings, of course, but sometimes family doesn't really understand. It was a very hard struggle, and I had to go through it alone.

Because this book is about my faith journey, I am choosing to respect my former wife's dignity and personhood and not share personal details about her or about our relationship. I don't feel that it glorifies God in any way to dwell on past pains and hurts. Divorce is never easy, for the couple divorcing, their children, or other family members. Learning to live with a different family structure is challenging, but with God's grace and with a humble heart, God does help us to move forward.

My close friends who weren't Catholic suggested that I start dating once I was divorced. They meant well, but that was not what I needed or what I was looking for at the time. Also, this would have gone against the teaching of the Church, because even when the divorce is final, a couple is still married in the eyes of the Church until an annulment is granted. We did go through the annulment process, and though it took several years, the annulment was granted.

The annulment process can be a time of healing for some, but it is still difficult. Thanks be to God that the Church has updated the annulment process so that couples can receive the adjudication from the Church in a timely manner.

I continued to go to prayer meetings because those meetings were an important part of my life and were a great support to me. In spite of all the pain and turmoil, I knew that the Holy Spirit was guiding me to continue my faith journey.

God is merciful. If I had been married before I was ordained, I would not have been able to marry again. My state in life would have been as a celibate deacon. Some need to be married; I think I am one of those people.

There is an appointed time for everything,
and a time for every affair under the heavens.
(Ecclesiastes 3:1)

✤ God's Grace

Change can be difficult, but even if it's good, change is inescapable. Sometimes we are forced to make changes, and sometimes we are the force behind the changes. Perhaps you have had to make changes in your life that were difficult. How did you cope? What was your prayer life like during those times? What did you learn that you can pass on to others who are facing difficult changes?

Take some time to write down what you've learned. This can be anything from how you handled people who were insensitive to your suffering or asked too many questions to specific ways God sustained you in prayer. As you consider what you've learned, ask yourself if there is a ministry you can join in your parish in which you could serve others using the wisdom you have gained.

As difficult situations arise in your life, turn to God in prayer. Pray for God's peace to envelop you during the situation. Our peace comes not from the world or what is or is not happening around us; rather, our peace is from Jesus.

CHAPTER THIRTY-TWO

GOD'S PLAN

God has our lives so intimately planned. Years ago, I knew a woman at church, but I didn't know that she had a daughter. I could not, therefore, have guessed that this woman would ultimately become my mother-in-law. After I met her beautiful daughter, Andi, in church, things slowly progressed, and we began dating. I really wasn't looking for anyone. I was doing ministry at the time.

While Andi and I were dating, we had many serious discussions. Neither of us wanted anything but a solid, faith-filled partner. She was strong in her faith, and I was striving to be a man of God. She was a teacher with a master's degree in education and supervision. She doesn't teach today but plans to go back and get a master's in divinity or in Scripture one day. She is a beautiful woman with a striking, quiet spirit. My children love her and are respectful to her. She is a good, solid person. We have one son together. We will be married seventeen years in June 2018.

Although I still wanted to be a deacon, there were obstacles. In order for a married man to be a deacon in the Catholic Church, he has to be married for at least five years. So I continued to learn and grow in my faith. In 2008 I spoke to the archbishop, and he accepted me back into the diaconate program. I was ordained a deacon at St. Louis King of France Cathedral in New Orleans on December 13, 2008.

My ordination was a very emotional experience for me. I recalled all that I had been through in experiencing God's amazing grace. I thought of the slaves who had been sold in Congo Square, less than two miles from where I was ordained. I thought of the hundreds of thousands of black people who were sold and suffered and died in New Orleans. In that same city, very close to where my ancestors were held as slaves, the archbishop laid his hands on me in prayer.

Find your delight in the LORD
 who will give you your heart's desire. (Psalm 37:4)

God's Grace

One way to grow in your spiritual life is to have a strong awareness of God. Noticing the ways that God is present in your life will help you develop that awareness. As you begin to see the movements of God in your life, you need to start "stepping into" them through "agreement" prayer. Praying in agreement with God is essential.

In this type of prayer, you state what you believe God is doing in your life, what God wants to do in your life, and then agree with God that you want to help with that movement. One type of agreement prayer that is communal as well as individual is the Our Father. When you pray this prayer, you say, "Thy kingdom come, thy will be done." You are praying that God's will be accomplished, not your own. We pray this prayer to bring that kingdom reality to earth.

Start practicing agreement prayer in your personal prayer time. It will help you to focus on what God is calling you to do, so that you can serve him more intentionally and with less distraction.

CHAPTER THIRTY-THREE

MY MOTHER

My mom knew a lot sooner than I did that I was called to ministry. Apparently, several people in my family knew it. My older brother Cliff and my brother George knew it. From what they have shared with me, they thought I had a calling on my life to preach the Word of God.

A man who lived near our house on the plantation nicknamed me "Preacher" when I was a boy. He called me Preacher because I would stand on a stump and curse like a sailor in a litany of curses. He said, "That boy's *gonna* be a preacher." Don't ask me how he came to this conclusion. I suppose that others can see the goodness in us even when we cannot see it in ourselves.

I fondly remember Mom's seventy-fifth birthday. The entire family was gathered to honor her on that evening, and I was chosen to be the emcee to keep things going. Mom had a way of making everyone want to be around her, and of course, everyone was invited. I do mean *everyone*—the in-laws, former in-laws, former spouses of children, neighbors, and many other people whose lives she had touched.

Many stood and gave witness to Mom's impact on their lives over many years, despite her apparent limitations in education and financial resources. They testified about how Mom had quietly given food when she had little herself, or of how she had encouraged someone who had troubles. Mom was an encourager and a fighter! She had a humble dignity about her, and when she shared about her struggles, with her voice trembling, I was moved by the power of the spirit of perseverance and faith that the Lord had given her.

We all gathered around, listening intently to her every word. There was no doubt the Lord had protected and provided for her and her family and the many others he sent into her life. We knew then that we would not have Mom in our midst for many more years. But that evening she was with us, and the power of God's grace pressing down on her and into her life was a powerful witness to everyone.

Mom didn't make it to my ordination, but she came to my first Mass. Five months after I was ordained, she died. At her funeral, they sang "I'll Fly Away." The funeral was truly what is known in the black Baptist Church as a "home going."

It was a beautiful thing to see: black people, white people, and her large family all together. It was amazing. We celebrated her life and the gift that she was to us. She was a faith-filled woman. She was a great cook. She ministered to all of her daughters-in-law in the family. She taught my wife how to make her special gumbo. She was an all-around good woman. So many young women were naturally attracted to her goodness. In addition, many young men like my nephews went to her for counsel. She was always an encourager.

Whenever I was having a rough time or struggling with some issue, I would go and sit in the simple little house where she lived, and she would say, "It's gonna be alright, Son." Just those effortless words of faith, which were part of her ministry, comforted me and countless others. Mom always had a word of faith. That was my mom. She was a strong woman—emotionally and spiritually.

Well over a thousand people came to her funeral and packed into the small Baptist church, filling it to overflowing. Mom never drove a car or traveled much, but she managed to touch people's lives literally all over the country.

Blessed are they who mourn,
for they will be comforted. (Matthew 5:4)

✿ God's Grace

It's important to have a spiritual mentor, someone who has been on a similar faith journey as you and can help you walk your own journey of faith. I say similar faith journey because everyone is different, and God communicates with each of us in different ways. The ways in which we perceive God and react to God are different as well.

A mentor doesn't need to be older than you or have had a wide-ranging experience of the world. A good mentor is someone who has wisdom and the gift of encouragement. A few things to look for when choosing a mentor: does the potential mentor have spiritual gifts similar to yours, lead a Spirit-filled life, want to be a mentor, and feel called to be a mentor to you at this time?

A good spiritual mentor is someone who will encourage you to step out in faith to answer the call of God on your life. It is someone who will be there for you as a spiritual guide or sounding board in the areas in which you want to grow. Spiritual mentors usually have a "season" during which they help us, and then we may change to another mentor for a different season. God sends people into our lives—throughout our lives—who will encourage, guide, teach, train, gently correct, and mentor us in our spiritual growth.

CHAPTER THIRTY-FOUR

JUSTICE AND MERCY

As a young man, I wanted justice. However, I wanted justice the way that human beings want it. I heard a young preacher teach about mercy and justice. "Mercy is greater than justice," he said, and this is the story he told:

Justice said to Mercy, "Let's have a meeting at three o'clock at Jacob's well. Don't you be late." Mercy said, "Don't worry, Justice; I'll be there right on time."

Justice got to Jacob's well first, and he was walking around the well. Suddenly, Justice became stuck in quicksand. (See, sometimes Justice gets stuck.) Justice was going down for the count; he was up to his knees, then up to his waist, and then up to his neck. The more he struggled, the deeper in he got. Justice was going down in the quicksand and about to be snuffed out. He cried out, "Oh, Mercy, where art thou?"

Mercy was nowhere to be seen. One last time, Justice cried out, "Oh, Mercy!"

Suddenly, Justice felt the hand of Mercy on his hand. Mercy pulled Justice out of the quicksand. Justice washed himself off and said, "Mercy, where were you when I called out to you?"

Mercy said, "Oh, Justice, I heard you calling out to me. I was on my way to help you, and I heard my friends Shadrach, Meshach, and Abednego. They were in the fiery furnace, and I had to get in that fiery furnace and fan the flames. I'm sorry that I smell like smoke, but I had to help those three Jewish boys.

"When I heard you cry out, I was on my way to help you, and then I heard my friend Daniel in the lions' den. And ol' Mercy had to get in the lions' den and close up the mouths of the lions. I'm sorry that my clothes are a little bit torn.

"Finally, I was on my way to help you, and then I heard Moses. He was down at the Red Sea, backed up against the wall. The Egyptians were hot on his trail. I went down to the Red Sea and fanned the waves with the other side of my garment, and I caused a wall of water to stand on either side so that Moses and the Israelites could pass through on dry land. I'm sorry; I got a little bit wet.

"Then I heard your cry, and I got on the wings of Goodness and Kindness and flew quickly and came here and pulled you out of the quicksand."

Justice said, "I see how it is with you, Mercy. You may not come when I want you, but you're always right on time."

Yes, I was demanding justice as a young angry black man, but God's mercy is indeed greater than justice. I understood that truth when I heard that story. God was building precept upon precept for me, truth upon truth, with the Indian chief story and with the story of Justice and Mercy. Those are part of me now. They will forever be part of me.

I minister in a city that, at the height of the slave trade in the 1700s, held more slaves than any other city in the United States. As I've said, slaves were sold in Congo Square, an open space within Louis Armstrong Park in the Tremé neighborhood, just across Rampart Street and north of the French Quarter. Men, women, and children suffered here in this square that I pass by on my way home every time I leave the cathedral.

This past that I was not part of echoes in my mind whenever I come near that section of the city. It is very powerful!

For sin is not to have any power over you, since you are not under the law but under grace. (Romans 6:14)

God's Grace

As you pray for God's mercy for your life, notice that you may be able to offer mercy to someone else. Have you ever prayed for something simple, like a good parking space, and praised God for his kindness when you receive a spot right up front? That same day, did you choose to let someone merge in front of your car when you were stuck in a long line of traffic? Did you show that person kindness and mercy by letting them in? This is a simple example, but when we give and receive mercy, even in small ways in our daily lives, we build our "mercy muscle."

God is both merciful and just, but we, his followers, often have an easier time demanding justice and a harder time demonstrating mercy. Both are necessary, but as Jesus said to his disciples, "Be merciful, just as . . . your Father is merciful" (Luke 6:36).

Go and learn the meaning of the words, "I desire mercy, not sacrifice." (Matthew 9:13)

CHAPTER THIRTY-FIVE

AMBASSADOR

As Christians, we are ambassadors of God's love, grace, and mercy. An ambassador is someone who represents a nation or another person. We are ambassadors for Jesus Christ—that is, God is appealing to people through us as we participate in the common priesthood of Jesus Christ.

No, it is not easy to fulfill this job, because if you are a Christian, you are on the job 24/7. I am always a deacon, for example, but more important, I am always a person who represents Christ. Yes, I guess this is the job that I have been searching for all my life. I am privileged; this is the greatest job that anyone can have!

Some people think that being a Christian is boring or pointless, but really, it is a great work, because we are aiming for eternal life in the presence of God. That's not a fairy tale. If we are faithful, Jesus will bring us to the house of the Father in the Parousia, at the end of time. I believe with all my heart that the Lord will come again in glory.

No one knows when the Lord will return. "But of that day and hour no one knows, neither the angels of heaven, nor the Son, but the Father alone" (Matthew 24:36). The First Letter to the Thessalonians completes the picture of how that return might look:

For the Lord himself, with a word of command, with the voice of an archangel and with the trumpet of God, will come down from heaven, and the dead in Christ will rise first. Then we who are alive, who are left, will be caught up

together with them in the clouds to meet the Lord in the air.
(1 Thessalonians 4:16-17)

I want to be in that number when Jesus comes.

I hold dear the knowledge that I have been given the privilege to minister the gospel. I treasure this great responsibility. I know that with God and with the power of his Holy Spirit, given to me at baptism and confirmation and in numerous infillings, I can do it. God fills us repeatedly to overflowing with his Holy Spirit, equipping us to do the work he gives us. I am dependent upon that to execute my charge, as a minister of the gospel and as a Christian.

I am awed and overwhelmed by God's mercy and his grace, because I was a sinner, and I still am. I didn't know that I was a sinner until God's grace invaded my sinfulness and set me free from bondage. The Letter to the Romans famously says that "the wages of sin is death" (Romans 6:23), and yet we live because of God's grace and his mercy.

God is sometimes called "the Hound of Heaven"; a well-known poem by that name captures God's unfailing search for each of us, no matter how we try to hide from him. He is always looking for us. He is always looking! His sovereign act of looking for us is an act of his grace. In other words, he invades our space. We can reject the grace that God offers. Nevertheless, he invades our space and comes into our lives.

God is always knocking at the door of our hearts. And like the telephone commercial, God is always asking, "Can you hear me now? Can you hear me now?" He does that through people. He does that through circumstances. He did it for me. He actually used race and racism in reverse to bring me to his own bosom. How awesome is this God of ours?

Yes, because God has invaded me with his grace, he invites me to look at everybody the way that he does. I don't always do that perfectly, but still he says, *These are my created ones. I fashioned them with my own hands. I blew my breath into them. One may look different. One may have a better tan or a little less tan, but they are all mine. My breath is in all of them.*

You cannot be a racist or be prejudiced and be a child of God. Such hatred is simply incongruent with Christianity; it is not part of God's kingdom. I struggled to ask God to forgive me for my past, and through Jesus' death on the cross, God's love washed away my sinful past. Scripture says that "without the shedding of blood there is no forgiveness" (Hebrews 9:22), and so the omnipotent, omniscient, omnipresent, and all-loving God sent his own Son to become the sacrifice. Instead of seeing the sin in my life, God sees the blood of the Lamb, his Son, Jesus Christ.

I feel similar to how John Newton must have felt. Newton was a crew member on board a slave ship in the 1700s, bringing slaves to England. One day there was a great storm upon the sea, and the ship nearly went down. Newton was sure that not only the ship but the cargo of slaves and his own life would be lost. As the storm raged and the ship tossed to and fro, Newton prayed for the first time in years. Much later, meditating on that storm on the sea and his own personal storms—he lived a degenerate life and continued in the slave trade for several more years—John Newton wrote a great hymn well-known to Christians and non-Christians alike: "Amazing Grace."

I was lost, like John Newton. I was stuck in the slavery, if you will, of misery and hatred. That was my trade. I was blind: I could only see through the eyes of hatred and through the eyes of race. But God delivered me. His grace overwhelmed me, caught me, and removed the scales from my eyes. I could say, like John Newton,

"Amazing grace! How sweet the sound that saved a wretch like me! I once was lost, but now am found; was blind, but now I see."

It feels good to be found by God. I am still searching for more of God's grace and more of his light. I know that I am dependent on God's mercy and his continual forgiveness. I know that I have been forgiven, I am being forgiven, and I will be forgiven.

As it says in the Book of Revelation,

They conquered him [the Devil] by the blood of the Lamb
and by the word of their testimony;
love for life did not deter them from death.
(Revelation 12:11)

And to what do we testify? It is this: that Christ has died, Christ has risen, and Christ will come again. That is our testimony.

John Newton's story resonates in me. Those hopeless black souls in the belly of the ship put in my mind my life without hope on the plantation. Those slaves, those black souls in the belly of the ship, were far greater in number than the white captors on deck. But the crew members, though few in number, were equipped with guns and chains, allowing them to control their "cargo."

God's amazing grace has helped me overcome race. But we still have a deep divide in race relations, not only in New Orleans, but in our nation. I do not want any of my black brothers or sisters to think that I am naive because, through God's mercy, I have begun to overcome the power of race in my life and no longer see color before person. I understand that racism is still a significant issue in our city and our nation.

I refuse to be a victim by giving in to the power of hate. I believe that God's love is greater than race. I have experienced his overwhelming grace, which has helped me overcome the power of race.

And his amazing grace has not only helped me overcome race but has shown me that his Son, Jesus Christ, is his gift to the world and his personal gift to me as well.

> *Blessed those who keep his testimonies,*
> *who seek him with all their heart.*
> *They do no wrong;*
> *they walk in his ways. (Psalm 119:2-3)*

☙ God's Grace

Archbishop Gregory Aymond of New Orleans wrote this prayer for the people of New Orleans, asking God to help us overcome violence, murder, and racism. It is a fitting prayer with which to conclude my story, reminding us that all people of goodwill are called to work and pray for an end to the evils of racial prejudice:

> *Loving and faithful God, through the years the people of our archdiocese have appreciated the prayers and love of Our Lady of Prompt Succor in times of war, disaster, epidemic, and illness. We come to you, Father, with Mary our Mother, and ask you to help us in the battle of today against violence, murder, and racism.*
>
> *We implore you to give us your wisdom, that we may build a community founded on the values of Jesus, which gives respect to the life and dignity of all people.*
>
> *Bless parents, that they may form their children in faith. Bless and protect our youth, that they may be peacemakers of our time. Give consolation to those who have lost loved ones through violence.*

Hear our prayer, and give us the perseverance to be a voice for life and human dignity in our community.

We ask this through Christ our Lord. Amen.

Our Lady of Prompt Succor, hasten to help us.

Mother Henriette Delille, pray for us, that we may be a holy family.

Hope and Purpose Ministries

Through prayer and discernment with my wife and a few trusted spiritual friends, I founded Hope and Purpose Ministries to proclaim the kingdom of God, encourage others that God has a plan and purpose for their lives, and help heal the brokenhearted. The Scriptures that are the foundation of Hope and Purpose Ministries are

As you go, make this proclamation: "The kingdom of heaven is at hand." (Matthew 10:7)

For I know well the plans I have in mind for you . . . plans for your welfare and not for woe, so as to give you a future of hope. (Jeremiah 29:11)

I came so that they might have life and have it more abundantly. (John 10:10)

In support of our mission statement and core Scriptures, Hope and Purpose Ministries has five main initiatives: Prayer, New Evangelization, Urban Evangelization, International Evangelization, and Ecumenical Harmony.

I believe that Hope and Purpose Ministries is my divine assignment on earth. God has truly gifted me with amazing grace to take me from the plantation to where I am today. God took me from a place of injustice and despair to a place that offers hope to others. He has lifted me up and turned me around so that now I too can sing, "I'll fly away" and know exactly to whom I am flying.

For we do not preach ourselves but Jesus Christ as Lord. (2 Corinthians 4:5)

If you would like to learn more about Hope and Purpose Ministries, please visit our website, www.HopeAndPurpose.org.

Deacon Larry Oney is a permanent deacon for the Archdiocese of New Orleans, serving at Divine Mercy Parish in Kenner, Louisiana. He is the founder and president of Hope and Purpose Ministries.

Deacon Oney is also the chairman of HGI Global, a risk management and project management firm headquartered in New Orleans. He is married to Andi, a fellow evangelist, who collaborates with him in ministry. Deacon Oney's dynamic preaching style and message of hope and purpose have led him to ministry engagements across the globe—from Europe to Africa to Brazil to Canada and throughout the United States. He serves on the board of directors for Renewal Ministries and on the board of trustees for Franciscan University, and he is a member of the New Orleans chapter of Legatus.

Deacon Oney is the author of *Reflections on the Kingdom of God; UP FAITH! God loves a faith that is always looking up!;* and *Your Divine Mission: Discovering, Entering, and Walking in Your Divine Mission*. He coauthored with Fr. William Maestri *Preaching Jesus in the Time of the New Evangelization*.